# TRUE CRIME

## UNSOLVED

From The Case Files of

## Claire Welch

# Contents

Introduction     vi

## Murders

**Rose Harsent**     1

**Emily Dimmock**     5

**Marion Gilchrist**     13

**Caroline Luard**     21

**Joseph Wilson**     27

**Bella Wright**     30

**Janet Smith**     35

**Julia Wallace**     39

**Sir Harry Oakes**     43

**Charles Walton**     47

**Betty Short**     52

**The Somerton Man**     57

**Emily Armstrong**     62

**The Boy in the Box**     65

**Wendy Sewell**     70

**Eve Stratford**     74

**Renee and Andrew MacRae**     81

**Bob Crane**     84

**Genette Tate**     87

**Carl Bridgewater**   99

**Suzy Lamplugh**   104

**Linda Cook**   115

**Elaine Doyle**   120

**Julie Ward**   124

**Sandy Drummond**   130

**Lindsay Jo Rimer**   132

**Melanie Hall**   134

**Billie-Jo Jenkins**   139

**Jill Dando**   142

# Multiple Deaths

**Brighton Trunk Murders**   158

**Jack the Stripper and the Hammersmith Murders**   170

**The Lake Bodom Murders**   181

**Bible John**   185

**The Monster of Florence**   190

**The Zodiac Killer**   198

**Babes in the Wood Killings**   206

# Introduction

Despite the fact that many people living in poorer communities at the beginning of the 20th century had little, or no, faith in or respect for the police, the Victorians had a long-held belief that crime could, and would, be beaten. Statistics published throughout the second half of the 19th century alluded to the fact that crime rates were falling. Violent crime was certainly being taken far more seriously than it had been in previous centuries, and perpetrators were severely dealt with by the courts.

By the turn of the 20th century, police forces had been steadily improving for almost 50 years. They were successful in suppressing forms of behaviour that polite society considered offensive and they had generally brought about some order and control. However, a number of factors continued to affect crimes throughout the 20th century, including government, war, the economy, beliefs and technology. Britain's industrial supremacy was in decline, with national unemployment reaching 22 per cent by 1933; in parts of Scotland, Wales and northern England, the figures were considerably higher. And, while new industries in car manufacturing, radio, household goods and electricity began to go from strength to strength, some of the population went without work for 20 years or more. This was brought about by two fundamental factors. There was a huge contrast in wealth and poverty between classes and people had to move hundreds of miles in search of work. As a result, communities became far less stable than they had been and neighbours were often unknown. However, other factors began to improve life for the nation as a whole.

When the Liberal government (1906–1914) introduced the "Welfare State", it was no longer likely that members of the public would starve to death or die in total poverty. Free medical care was introduced through the National Health Service and education became available to all children up to the age of 16. Greater security was enjoyed by all, while new laws outlawing sex and race discrimination were introduced. The First World War (1914–1918) and the Second World War (1939–1945) brought about further changes to people's lives through conscription, evacuation, and the destruction of cities and towns. At the same time, there was less influence from the church, and religious beliefs began to decline; attitudes were more likely to be shaped by newspapers, radio and, eventually, television. In addition, new innovations had an effect on crime: aeroplanes made international smuggling easier, and car crime became a hot topic. Smuggling contraband in the early part of the century usually involved gin, brandy and cigarettes. Today, smuggling human beings into the UK is big business.

By the end of the 20th century, technological advances and the widespread use of the computer and the World Wide Web would introduce the population to cybercrime, which is becoming ever-more complicated and sophisticated. Statistically, two-thirds of all crimes are committed by males under the age of 25 (females are outnumbered seven to one), while half of all crimes are committed by men under 20 years of age. Young males, in the 15–16 age group, are most likely to commit a crime. With better health care, increased education and the possibility of greater prosperity throughout the second half of the 20th century and into the 21st century, it is perhaps hard to see why anyone would want to commit a crime – or is it? Lifestyles may have changed and, apart from the fact that Britain has suffered a huge economic downturn since 2008, with crimes involving property and possessions on the increase and a country bound by recession, prosperity is far greater than it was more than 100 years ago. However, in December 2011 unemployment reached a peak, with the highest number of young people out of work for 17 years. With the suspension and abolition of capital punishment in the second half of the 20th century, deterrents have changed (although serious punishments still exist for the most heinous crimes), but human nature itself is unlikely to change significantly enough to end all crime. Jealously, greed, obsession, cruelty, fear, mental states of mind and peer pressure will all still continue to challenge, excite and stimulate those who perpetrate crimes.

Criminals have been perceived by groups in authority and the public in varying different ways throughout history. There were those who would equate a criminal offender as "working class", lazy, prone to drinking and looking for an easy life rather than willing to work for an honest wage. At the turn of the 19th century, others were termed as "dangerous" for taking advantage of disorder within the slums, and up to the early 1900s "criminal classes" had a term all of its own. However, with changes in social understanding and developments in the world of psychiatry, it became increasingly clear that criminals were individuals who were suffering from various forms of behavioural

Unsolved

abnormalities brought about by either nature or nurture. With changing attitudes in almost every aspect of life throughout the 20th century, policing and the public's attitude to the police changed dramatically. At the turn of the century, there were 181 police forces and 60,000 police officers in Britain. Many forces were small, with less than 50 policemen, and there was very little collaboration or co-operation between the different forces. There was also no central criminal record base but, slowly, developments did begin to take place. The use of new technology saw police forces amalgamating, and by the beginning of the new millennium there were 125,000 police officers working in 41 forces across Britain. The job today remains much as it did in 1900 but technology has greatly increased the role of the police, and they now have a far better chance of bringing criminals to justice. New technology, including fingerprinting (developed in 1901) and DNA testing (first reported in 1984 and developed as a process ever since), have created important new ways to identify criminals.

Collating information is crucial in identifying perpetrators of crime, and the age of computing opened up huge opportunities for holding and analysing such information. Today, the National Police Computer holds records on more than 25 million people, searchable in a variety of ways. However, despite greater uniformity across police forces (although a Home Office report in December 2011 found that there are huge improvements that could be made in this area), huge databases, collaboration and technological advances, crimes still blot the landscape of British society. Those that remain unsolved, especially heinous crimes, are particularly upsetting, intolerable for both victims and their families, and provide a constant source of frustration to the authorities working towards capturing those responsible. Unsolved crimes, or "cold cases" as they are also known, are an unsettling and worrying fact of life. This is further compounded by the fact that the Forensic Science Service – a critical resource – has an unsecure future. The evidence provided by the Forensic Science Service is the only hope of solving many "cold cases", including killings and rapes, dating back decades and committed across Britain. The vast archive of evidence includes thousands of items from crime scenes, such as clothing, body fluids, hair, shoes and microscopic splatters, all of which are needed for DNA profiling. It is currently being considered whether the National Policing Improvement Agency should take over the archive – currently housed in London and the Midlands – but with the agency due for closure in December 2012, it is unclear how secure the resource will be. If there is no suitable organization or department available with the expertise or resources to take on the archive, it seems likely that unsolved crimes will not only continue to blight society, they might also increase – a far cry from beating crime.

# Murders

## Rose Harsent

(Peasenhall Murder, 1902)

Providence House, which sits on a long straggling street in the middle of the village of Peasenhall, Suffolk, just 30 miles from Ipswich, was the scene of a mysterious murder at the end of May 1902. Unmarried 23-year-old Rose Harsent was found dead in the kitchen of the house, where she worked as a servant, by her distraught father. Despite two men (one of whom was tried twice) being suspected of her murder, the case remains unsolved.

Approaching midnight on the night of 31st May 1902 – the time that Harsent was known to have been murdered – there was a terrible thunderstorm. Just two hours before, Harsent, who was six months' pregnant, had been seen signalling with a light from an upper window on the right of the house. To whom she was signalling is unknown; however, it was reported that in 1901 Harsent had had an affair with William Gardiner, some 12 years her senior, who was married with six children. Local gossips believed at the time that Harsent was signalling to Gardiner, who was believed to be the father of her unborn baby: his small semi-detached cottage lay within sight of Providence House.

The case began with police suspecting that Harsent had committed suicide due to her difficult circumstances; however, the victim's throat had been cut and there had been an attempt to burn the body using petroleum. Following a different line of questioning, the police quickly established the victim's former relationship with Gardiner, a Primitive Methodist preacher and foreman of Smyth's, a local seed drill works, and quickly arrested the 35-year-old. Gardiner's case was probably not helped by local gossip, which had led to a hearing within his church, where he was admonished for impropriety.

At his first trial, presided over by Sir William Grantham in 1902, Gardiner was defended by Henry Fielding Dickens. Despite the best efforts of prosecutor Ernest Wild, the jury was unable to reach a verdict, with an 11 to one split in favour of "guilty". At Gardiner's second trial in 1903, in which there was further prosecution evidence, he was again defended by Fielding Dickens, and prosecuted by Wild, who was renowned for his "eloquent and impassioned speeches" (often seemingly able to hypnotize members of the jury); however, the second jury also failed to reach a verdict. But, this time, the 12-strong jury formed a verdict of 10 to two of "not guilty". It was to be the end of Gardiner's involvement in the case and the prosecution went on to issue a writ of *nolle prosequi*, meaning "to be unwilling to pursue". This basically signified that the prosecution was willing to voluntarily discontinue the case, and it left Gardiner as one of the few people in English history to have been tried for murder twice with no verdict returned.

However, events took a different turn two years after Harsent's murder when artilleryman Taylor – a military prisoner at Dover – confessed to the killing to his prison governor, Major Daniels. At first, the news was treated sceptically by locals and the authorities alike, but the fact that Taylor – whose real identity was never fully established – was adamant in his written confession, and the fact that he had enlisted at Ipswich did give some weight to his story.

On hearing that Taylor had confessed to the killing, the shadow that had hung over Gardiner's life for two long years visibly shifted. His face brightened, and he fervently exclaimed: "It seems too good to be true, although I have trusted and hoped that the truth would be known before my life ended. There is nothing for me to do but wait. And I shall be grateful – only God knows how grateful – if the dreadful mystery is cleared up."

With a string of offences on his record, Taylor had left Peasenhall in Suffolk under a cloud in January or February 1903, when his then employer accused him of petty theft. It was known that he joined the Militia before enlisting in the Regulars some three months later. However, the facts of the murder were not quite as straightforward as Taylor claimed, and despite his repeated confessions of guilt, he failed to satisfy the detective force at Ipswich that he was the murderer.

Although Taylor's story was plausible overall, when answering questions from Superintendent Staunton – the man in charge of the investigation – it fell to pieces in terms of any real details. It was deduced by Ipswich police that Taylor was suffering from melancholy (like many soldiers undergoing sentences in military prisons) and that the artilleryman was merely seeking a change in circumstances and a change in punishment. Major Daniels stated to the Ipswich police that the self-confessed murderer was extremely calm when telling his story and fully realized the severe gravity of the crime he was adamant he had committed. However, Taylor further proved his innocence when, asked how he had managed to fund his trip from Ipswich to London, he claimed that he: "... put my hand in the dead girl's pocket and took out a half-sovereign, a five-shilling piece, and two half-crowns. She was wearing a black dress." However, it was established at the time of the murder that Harsent had been wearing nothing but her nightdress and some stockings. When confronted by the endless list of offences he had previously committed, Taylor stated: "I never had a chance; I was badly brought up."

The case was re-examined in detail in the television programme *Julian Fellowes Investigates: A Most Mysterious Murder*, where Fellowes speculates that it was likely that Harsent was killed by her former lover's jealous wife. Once the trials were over in Ipswich, Gardiner and his wife moved from the area to start a new life and began running a sweet shop. He died in 1941 without ever having been formally acquitted of the murder of the pregnant servant girl.

# Emily Dimmock

(Camden Town Murder, 1907)

The murder of 22-year-old Emily Dimmock became a sensation in 1907, in part due to the theatrical performances that were delivered in the courtrooms of the day, and partly because it was a landmark case in legal history. More than 100 years later, the case is still one of the most famous unsolved crimes of the 20th century, following interest from American crime writer Patricia Cornwell and her theories on Jack the Ripper, and artist Walter Sickert.

Emily Dimmock – also known as Mrs Shaw and Phyllis Dimmock – lived at 29 St Paul's Road, near King's Cross, with her partner Bertram "Bert" Shaw. She was found there on the morning of 12th September, lying almost naked across the bed with a cut to her throat that was so deep it had almost severed her head from her body. In addition, there were odd cuts across both her knees. It was quickly established that, due to a "cast-iron" alibi, Bert Shaw was not a suspect in the case. In fact, Shaw had a job working as a chef for the Midland Railway's night express and was away from home between 4.15pm until around 11.30am the following day. He was known to have stayed overnight in Sheffield before travelling back to the capital. Therefore, the police focused their investigation elsewhere.

Dimmock was a young woman who began her working life in service in East Finchley, Hertfordshire. Like many other young girls of her generation she found herself in King's Cross, north London, a renowned hotspot for prostitutes and drug dealers alike. Here, she lodged with small-time criminal John William Crabtree, who was charged with running a disorderly house just off the Euston Road in Bidborough Street. Dimmock was working as a prostitute when she moved in with Shaw early in 1907. It is known that the young Shaw – he was around 19 years old – was keen for Dimmock to give up her life as a prostitute. By day, Dimmock lived the life that Shaw desired for her but, when he was away at night, she returned to her former life of prostitution without his knowledge.

When glass-work designer Robert Wood posted a postcard to "Phyllis" in the early hours of Monday 9th September, signing it "Alice" so as not to arouse Shaw's suspicions, it was to make him central to the police case. Dimmock and Wood had met on the previous Friday at the Eagle in Royal College Street, where he wrote on the postcard to Dimmock, asking her to meet him at 8.15pm at the Rising Sun (he actually drew an artist's impression of a rising sun). Meanwhile, Dimmock spent three nights in a row with ship's cook Robert Percival Roberts. When she turned up at the Eagle on the evening of Wednesday 11th September, not far away, in the Rising Sun, Roberts was drinking with his friend Frank Clarke. The two men were expecting Dimmock to meet them. That night Dimmock was seen by several witnesses drinking with Wood. Roberts would later testify that it was on the morning of the day before she died that the victim showed him a letter folded in four. It was reportedly from Bert Shaw, asking her to meet him that evening in the Eagle in Camden Town at 8.30pm, but the writing proved similar to that of Wood's postcard and the charred remains would ultimately prove indecipherable to the police. The drinking session was to be the last time Emily Dimmock was seen alive.

The following morning, Bert Shaw's mother travelled from Northampton to her son's rooms to meet with Emily. Mrs Shaw was less than pleased with her son's involvement with the young prostitute and the visit was not a social one. Mrs Shaw arrived at the house well before her son's shift on the night express had ended and knocked on the door. There was no answer. A neighbour, Mrs Stocks, allowed Shaw's mother to sit in the passage to wait for her son; when he arrived he borrowed a key to enter the rooms. It was then that the three of them discovered Emily's bloodstained body.

It was clear to the two shocked women and Bert Shaw that the rooms had been ransacked – Dimmock's postcard collection had been wrecked (Wood's postcard was not found at the scene) and whoever had murdered her had clearly washed their hands in the basin in the bedroom. When the police arrived they quickly began to piece together Dimmock's life while Shaw was away. Bert eventually found the postcard, which Emily Dimmock had carefully hidden, when he moved rooms and was clearing out her belongings. Wood was soon identified as the author. However, at best, the evidence against the designer was circumstantial and many men – particularly soldiers and sailors known to the victim – were questioned about the crime.

Two days after the murder, newspaper reports confirmed that a bloodstained man's handkerchief (showing a laundry mark) had been retrieved by police from the crime scene, along with a crumpled letter found under the bed and the charred remains of other correspondence from the fire. Reports also stated that many bloodstained fingerprints in the bedroom were found on the bedclothes, the bedposts and the washbasin. Fingerprinting was in its early stages and it was far too soon to use the process. "The room was in disorder, as if there had been a struggle" was the official description of the scene and it was this, along with the fact that jewellery belonging to the victim worth up to £10 had been stolen, that led police to believe initially that the motive had been robbery. However, the evidence possibly suggests something more sinister. Dimmock was found on the bed in a sleeping position, there were no defensive wounds to her arms and her hair had been pulled to one side. It has been medically proven that it is difficult to cut a throat when the victim is struggling. It seems likely that Dimmock was totally unaware she was about to be attacked, suggesting that she was asleep between 3.00am and 6.00am when, following examination of her stomach contents, the murder is deduced to have taken place.

Four days after the murder, newspaper reports talked about "important developments in connection with the grim mystery" and stated that the police, led by Assistant Commissioner Macnaghten and Superintendent Vedy, "are confident that they will be able to make an arrest before many hours have passed". Despite the victim's postcard collection being wrecked on the night of the tragedy, the remaining postcards were proving helpful to police in their quest for the murderer. By this time, the police no longer suspected that robbery was the motive – it had been deduced that the victim had been attacked while she slept – and jealousy or revenge were cited in the daily newspapers as possible new motives. The inquest opened at noon on 16th September at St Pancras Coroner's Court. Despite reports that the authorities were close to an arrest, by 23rd September none had yet been made, although detectives were convinced they knew the identity of the killer. However, on 7th October 1907, police had indeed made an arrest. It was reported in the *Daily Mirror* that "they have taken into custody Robert Thomas William George Cavers Wood, aged about 29". Wood was brought before Clerkenwell Police Court that same day.

Wood's arrest had been brought about through the *Daily Mirror*'s suggestion to Scotland Yard that the postcards written to the victim were reproduced in the daily newspapers. The handwriting on one of the postcards was recognized by Ruby Young, a former girlfriend of Wood's, who mentioned it to a friend. Young and Wood met following the reproduction of the postcards in the newspapers and he admitted that he did know Dimmock, although he was adamant that he was not with her on the night she was murdered. Young's friend had a journalist friend at the time, who arranged for her to speak to Detective Inspector Neill, the man in overall charge of the case.

When arrested, Wood, from King's Cross, admitted that he had written the postcard making an appointment with Emily Dimmock at the Rising Sun on the night before she was murdered. He denied that a further three cards also sent to Dimmock were anything to do with him. He gave a full account of his movements the night Emily Dimmock was murdered and claimed to have first heard of the murder two days after it was committed. Wood also stated that he had only ever met the victim twice and that he did not even know her name. He recounted how he had written the postcard to "Phyllis" at her request, after he offered it to her instead of the postcards that were being sold by a young boy in the pub, and that also at her request he signed it in her friend's name "Alice", as she told him: "in case my old man should see it". The appointment, he claimed, was bogus. He stated that he then saw Dimmock again a few days later on Monday 9th September, both in the Rising Sun and later that evening when she was stopped by a group of men.

Wood's younger brother backed up his story of what happened on the Wednesday night. "He was a methodical man," stated Wood's brother, who always "returned home between 10.30pm and midnight". His brother claims Wood never varied from this pattern, so it would have been impossible for him to be out when the victim was attacked. Despite having an alibi, however, Wood was charged on 7th October 1907 with murder, and remanded for eight days when bail was refused by the magistrate.

The inquest was resumed on 14th October 1907. Bert Shaw was the first to give evidence. He confirmed that various pieces of jewellery had gone missing from the property on the night of the murder, along with three keys. Shaw also stated the times of the trains he took to and from Sheffield on the days in question and was able to prove his alibi for the inquest. Detective Inspector Neill was the next witness. It was stated that Wood alleged that the first time he met Dimmock was on Friday 6th September, just six days before the murder. The inquest was adjourned for a week and Wood was once again remanded in custody.

The New Bailey's public gallery was filled with many actors, writers and artists of the day, just as keen to see the renowned, high-profile Edward Marshall Hall QC in action defending Wood as they were to see the accused himself. Marshall Hall was loved by the crowd, who hung onto his every word, despite the fact that the case for Wood's defence was somewhat bizarre and varied. Wood had gone to extraordinary lengths to ensure his alibi for the evening of 11th September in the face of evidence by Robert McCowan – a witness for the prosecution – who was asked to describe the man he had seen leaving 29 St Paul's Road at around 4.55am on the fateful morning of 12th September. McCowan believed he saw the accused, wearing a hard bowler hat, leaving the premises with his collar upturned, and walking slightly jerkily while keeping his left hand in his pocket. (Following a childhood accident resulting in a damaged finger, Wood was known for keeping his hand out of sight.) However, despite the fact that witnesses swore that the man they saw was Wood due to the manner of his walk, and the fact that John Crabtree also swore under oath that Wood had previously visited his premises several times in Bidborough Street, the case rested on visibility. As much as the prosecution said they could bring in witnesses to say Wood had a distinctive walk, Marshall Hall claimed he could bring in just as many to say he did not.

Marshall Hall claimed that when McCowan walked down St Paul's Road it would have been impossible to tell, without close inspection, if the man he saw that morning was Wood. William Westcott, a keen boxer with a swing to his walk, and also a resident of St Paul's Road, was on an early shift at St Pancras that morning and was in the road at the same time as McCowan. Marshall Hall argued that it was Westcott that McCowan had seen, and not the accused. The point about the distinctive walk was conceded. Even though Marshall Hall's summing-up was excellent, he still felt that Wood could be convicted of the crime. However, the judge instructed the jury that the prosecution had an unproven case and, after deliberating for 15 minutes, a "not guilty" verdict was returned.

Wood was the first accused man in a murder trial to give evidence on his own behalf following the Criminal Justice Bill (1905). It was a landmark case in English legal history, even though it seems likely that Wood lied under oath – if Crabtree and the prostitutes were telling the truth about his association with Dimmock – and was an unreliable witness.

# Marion Gilchrist

(1908)

At 82 years old, Marion Gilchrist was fully in charge of her faculties. Given her age, spinster Gilchrist, who shared her home with her live-in maid Helen Lambie, was frail and somewhat absent-minded at times, but nevertheless relatively healthy. It was known that she worried about the possibility of burglars, and kept the outer door leading to her flat in the residential quarter of Queen's Terrace, Glasgow, locked at all times. The year was 1908 and Glasgow's reputation for its gang crime and frequent murders was notorious. Most of the city's underbelly of crime was a world away from the life that Gilchrist lived, but her nervousness about the possibility of being robbed led her to joke to her neighbour in the flat below that should she ever need help she would knock three times on the floor. In fact, Gilchrist had knocked three times on the floor on previous occasions when she felt anything was wrong, and good friend and neighbour Arthur Adams had looked in on the fastidious and cultured Gilchrist to check on the situation. But, apart from the fact that the elderly lady's dog had been mysteriously poisoned some months before, nothing had ever been amiss.

On the evening of 21st December 1908, Helen Lambie left her employer reading at the dining table as she headed out of the flat just before 7.00pm to buy the evening papers. Within the 10 minutes it would take for the young woman to return, Gilchrist was to suffer a savage and shocking attack, which left her dead in a pool of blood, and sparked events that led to a notorious miscarriage of justice and a cover-up by the authorities.

It was assumed that the motive for the attack was robbery. Gilchrist was a wealthy woman who, it was established, had a number of pieces of jewellery hidden in her wardrobe. At around 7.00pm on the night of the attack, Adams was relaxing at home with his sister when he heard knocking on the ceiling of his apartment. As the number of knocks was more than three he wasn't unduly concerned, but decided to head up to Gilchrist's flat to check on the elderly lady. Hovering outside the door, Adams could hear a noise which sounded like the maid breaking sticks. As Adams was unaware that Lambie wasn't at home, he ventured back down to his own apartment, before being persuaded by his sister to go back upstairs and check once more on Gilchrist. Adams arrived back at the flat door at about the same time as Lambie and, as the maid unlocked the door, a stranger calmly walked past them both. It only took a few seconds for Lambie to find her employer lying in the dining room, battered about the head and upper body. The victim was still barely alive at this point, and died within seconds of being found, at which point Lambie cried out to Adams: "My mistress is murdered ... catch that man!"

According to newspaper reports at the time, the stranger had not aroused any suspicion as he calmly walked by but, on hearing Lambie's cries from the dining room, Adams flew after him and "ran down the stairs almost at the heels of the man, but the stranger fled and was soon out of reach". The street outside was ill-lit with many opportunities to fade away into the darkness. Adams was very unlikely to see, or be able to catch, the elderly spinster's attacker. However, 15-year-old Mary Barrowman had also seen a man in the vicinity of Queen's Terrace the night of the murder, and was questioned about the suspect by police. Back at the flat, it soon became clear that of the valuables on the premises (a large quantity of Gilchrist's diamonds were kept at her jewellers in Glasgow), only an expensive diamond brooch was missing. The intruder had managed to force open a box in the victim's bedroom and a number of papers, rings and gold watches were found on the floor. Despite the fact that the police were convinced the motive was robbery, many thousands of pounds' worth of jewellery had been left untouched. The murderer was more interested in the victim's private papers, locked away in the bedroom. Gilchrist was popular with a wide circle of friends, and the police, fearing a public outcry, were keen to act quickly. The fact that her dog had been poisoned prior to the fateful night led the authorities to believe that the attack was premeditated.

Both Adams and Lambie gave a description of the suspect to police and when, five days later, the police were tipped off about a diamond brooch being pawned by a man living nearby, they were confident that they had their man. Oscar Slater – originally Oscar Leschziner – was a German Jew who had fled to Glasgow in order to avoid military conscription. The fact that his life was particularly sordid – he was a pimp, trafficker of stolen jewellery and gambler – did little to help his cause with the police. Armed with their tip-off about the brooch, the police arrived at Slater's home – only to discover that he had recently left Scotland, bound for New York on the *Lusitania* under a false name

– Otto Sando – with his mistress Andree Antoine. With these new revelations, the police were more convinced than ever that Slater was the man for whom they were looking.

When the vessel docked in New York, Slater was arrested for murder by local detectives, who found a diamond brooch in the suspect's pocket. Adams, Lambie and Barrowman then crossed the Atlantic in order to identify Slater. Both Lambie and Barrowman claimed that Slater could have been the man they had seen on the night of the murder, although Adams was less sure. Despite the fact that extradition proceedings were started, Oscar Slater was so convinced that he wouldn't be convicted of a crime of which he steadfastly maintained he was innocent, that he returned to Scotland of his own free will. It was to prove a huge mistake for the 37-year-old who found that anti-Jewish sentiment and his lifestyle would all go against him. There were 98 witnesses for the prosecution when Slater came to trial in Edinburgh in early May 1909. Although, in New York, Helen Lambie had not been totally convinced that Slater was the murderer she saw in the flat, by the time the case came to trial the maidservant was adamant that the man she had seen on the night in question was the German. His case was further compounded by evidence from Constable Buen, who claimed to have seen Slater "in the street near Miss Gilchrist's house at about 9.00pm about a week before the murder". This was perhaps unsurprising, as Slater lived about four roads away from Miss Gilchrist, but this was never mentioned at the time.

Lord Advocate, Alexander Ure, was convinced that Slater should hang, and the jury were under no illusion that they should find the man before them, "with a twisted nose" as described at the time by Detective Trench, guilty. Slater was indeed found guilty by the 15-strong jury and sentenced to death by hanging on 27th May 1909. The fact that the brooch in Slater's pocket was his own and not that of the dead woman, the fact that he'd been invited to the US by a friend, and the fact that he had changed his name in order to avoid his estranged wife had little or no sway in his case. A further travesty was that it was quite obvious that, due to Gilchrist's nervousness, she would never have opened her door to a stranger. The attacker must have been someone the victim knew, as there was no sign of forced entry. Slater and the murdered lady were unknown to each other. Marion Gilchrist had been battered to death in her own home, her head bashed "with lightning-like rapidity" between 20 and 40 times, and someone would pay. That someone would be Slater.

The death of Marion Gilchrist and the subsequent arrest and conviction of Slater had caused a sensation throughout Scotland and beyond. Rumours were rife, including the idea that Slater was actually Gilchrist's long-lost son or that the victim had been a resetter (a receiver of stolen uncut diamonds). All such rumours were identified as false and unfounded, but the case was mysterious and caused unrest and speculation that the police were eager to quash.

Almost as soon as Slater was sentenced to death, a petition for clemency was started on his behalf and more than 20,000 signatures were collected. Just one day before the death penalty was to be carried out, Slater's sentence was reduced to life imprisonment and he was transferred to Peterhead jail. Slater maintained his innocence and some of his friends approached the author Sir Arthur Conan Doyle to see if his influence might help achieve some justice for the convicted man. Conan Doyle had read about the case in *Notable Scottish Trials* and was appalled that Slater had been convicted on such flimsy circumstantial evidence and suspicion, but getting the case back into the public interest would turn out to be a slow and lengthy process. Conan Doyle's book *The Case of Oscar Slater*, published three years after Slater's conviction, brought about numerous demands for a pardon or retrial, but the authorities refused to change the status quo. It seemed that Slater had very little choice but to wait out his days in prison. However, he was not forgotten by those convinced of his innocence and, over the next 15 years, various facts were uncovered which would lead to his eventual release and pardon.

Conan Doyle re-examined all the evidence presented at the trial and found it surprising that Lambie did not react at all when she was passed in the corridor of the flat by the attacker. It became quite clear that she had known the assailant and although she had possibly been quite surprised to see him in her mistress's home, she was not panicked by his presence, which led Conan Doyle to suspect that she knew all too well that it was not Slater. He found other witnesses, including Duncan McBrain, who saw Slater outside his own flat at the time of the murder, and 30-year-old Agnes Brown, who actually saw the murderer escape from Miss Gilchrist's building. It was not Oscar Slater. However, neither of these witnesses were called to testify at Slater's trial. Conan Doyle wanted to know why.

Central to the police's case was the idea that it was Slater's name and description in the paper that had prompted the convicted man to flee Glasgow under a false name. However, Doyle discovered that not only had Slater booked passage for himself and his mistress some six weeks before the murder, but that he was already on his way to New York when the paper was published. At the trial, a jewel hammer was presented as evidence of the murder weapon; however, Doyle was unconvinced that such a weapon could have caused such devastating injuries to the victim. Furthermore, Dr Adams, first called to the scene on the night of 21st December 1908 – yet also never called upon to give evidence – found that the weapon most likely to have been used on the victim was one of her own dining room chairs. At the scene, the left back leg and front right leg of the chair were found to have brain, hairs and blood stuck to them – a fact that was never introduced at court. Dr Adams quickly deduced that the murderer had knocked Miss Gilchrist to the ground, picked up the chair in which she had been sitting and hit her with it five or six times. Considering the injuries suffered by the victim, Dr Adams was also fairly confident that the murderer had jumped up and down on the body of Marion Gilchrist, such was the frenzied nature of the attack. What Conan Doyle also discovered was that when the forensic scientists arrived the following morning to work on the crime scene, the dining room chair had been cleaned and moved back to its original position. It was police procedure at the time to preserve all evidence at the crime scene so, while it was possible to concede that the chair had been moved accidentally, the fact it had also been cleaned was extremely suspicious.

Conan Doyle was keen to re-examine the testimony of Helen Lambie because it was clear that, between seeing Slater in New York and seeing him again at the trial, she had changed her witness statement. Conan Doyle also questioned the prosecution's attempts to link Slater as the man, a "watcher", who had been spotted outside the flat on several occasions leading up to the murder. Around 20 people identified Slater with varying degrees of certainty as the man who had been seen outside the flat prior to the attack, but many of the so-called witnesses contradicted each other and Conan Doyle concluded this evidence was a farce. Detective Trench eventually admitted that he had never believed Miss Lambie's identification of Slater; he was sacked without a pension for leaking documents to the press which hinted at a conspiracy.

Finally, after serving 18 years in prison for a murder he did not commit, Oscar Slater was pardoned by the Scottish Court of Criminal Appeal after all the new evidence was presented to the authorities.

For some time after the events, it was thought that Miss Gilchrist's nephew, Dr Francis Charteris, had killed the victim, but another candidate might have been Wingate Birrell, the fiancé of Helen Lambie. However, it was also known that Helen Lambie was expected to "make herself scarce" when Miss Gilchrist had business visitors, and that such visitors were fairly "shady" acquaintances who dealt in valuable jewellery of not altogether legitimate origin. Perhaps the murderer was one of them.

# Caroline Luard

(Seal Chart Murder, 1908)

Caroline Mary Luard was murdered on 24th August 1908 at an isolated summerhouse close to her home, Ightham Knoll, near Sevenoaks in Kent. The victim was hit over the head and shot, in what still remains today an unsolved case.

Caroline Luard had married Major-General Charles Edward Luard in 1875 and the couple had two sons, Charles Elmhirst Luard and Eric Dalbiac Luard, born in 1876 and 1878 respectively.

The couple had been living in Kent for around 30 years at the time of the murder, where they were known as "constant and devoted companions". They had been retired for 20 years and Luard had had a good reputation as a soldier. He had been involved in planned improvements for Newgate jail, and the building of the Household Cavalry barracks in Windsor, as well as the United Recreation Ground in Portsmouth. It is also thought that he was instrumental in the rearmament of Gibraltar before retiring with his wife to Ightham Knoll. He went on to serve as a Kent County Councillor and a Justice of the Peace. Luard also became a governor of Shipbourne School where he took on the role of Local Inspector of Art and Drawing. Despite his heavy commitments, the former soldier also formed the Patriotic Party in 1907 and recommended that all farmers were taught how to shoot, following the vulnerability of the British Army in the Second Boer War (1899–1902). Meanwhile, his wife Caroline was involved in charity work, and both were outstanding pillars of the community. Sadly, both sons were lost at a young age after they joined the British Army. The youngest, Eric, died in 1903 after contracting a fever while on service in Africa, while Charles died in France in 1914.

On the afternoon that she died, Caroline Luard, having taken a walk with her husband, said goodbye to him at around 3.00pm on a Kent country road before taking a private road towards her own home. The soon-to-be victim was expecting a visitor for tea, Mrs Stewart, the wife of a local solicitor and, having taken the exercise she wanted to prior to going on holiday, she headed home. Luard wanted to retrieve his golf clubs from the nearby golf links at Godden Green and said he would meet her later. Mrs Luard took a private road through a wicket gate at Seal Chart. Her journey would take her on a secluded route across the expansive estate of Frankfield, Seal Chart, home to the couple's friends Mr and Mrs Wilkinson, an elderly wealthy couple who had granted the Luards access to their land and to the summerhouse or casa, which was situated halfway between the two properties. The casa was often frequented by Caroline Luard, who was a welcome visitor. Apart from being used for occasional afternoon tea parties, the summerhouse and the surrounding area – to within three quarters of a mile – were out of bounds to all but a privileged few.

Major-General Luard set off on the one and a half mile walk to Godden Green and returned home via the main road, which was the shortest route to his home. He was spotted several times during the following hour by various witnesses who would later confirm his story of his whereabouts at the time his wife was murdered. He was surprised to find that his wife had not returned home and, as she was absent, had tea with her invited guest. At the time, Luard thought his wife might have changed her mind and decided to have tea with another friend; however, when his wife still did not appear, he set off with the couple's Irish terrier to retrace her steps. The road from the woods led up to the balcony of the summerhouse and it was here that he found his wife's body. The terrier immediately ran to its mistress and began licking her face before "crying" by her side. It was obvious to Luard that his wife had suffered a blow to the head followed by two gunshot wounds. The glove of her left hand had been forcibly removed and three valuable rings were missing, along with her purse.

Luard, aided by his butler, then made his way to the cottage of Wickham, the Wilkinsons' coachman. Annie Wickham hardly recognized Luard when he turned up at their door. His face was pale and drawn with acute grief while his body was bent and the man could barely speak. According to newspaper reports at the time Mrs Wickham is stated as saying: "I said that something terrible must have happened. He told me, and I sent for my husband, and they went back to the summerhouse together.

"At 3.15pm in the afternoon I heard three shots fired, but, beyond thinking it strange that firing should take place at that time, I attached no importance to the incident."

Mrs Wickham was not the only witness to have heard the three shots; they were also heard by gardener Daniel Kettel.

After a doctor and the police had been sent for, the body was taken to the Luards' house where a post-mortem examination was carried out. The chief constable of Kent, Colonel Warde, and Superintendent Taylor, alongside every available member of the Kent constabulary, was drafted to the case, but no clues were found as to whom the assailant might be. The police discounted the fact that it could just be an ordinary robbery – robbers of the day were not in the habit of carrying revolvers, which was by now known to have been the cause of death. In addition, the location of the summerhouse was so remote that it was thought unlikely that anyone would just stumble across it. Rather, the police believed that the attacker would have known Caroline Luard's movements and had waited close to the summerhouse in order to attack the unsuspecting victim.

The police strongly suspected that the robbery of the rings and purse was a rouse to throw them off the scent, but the Luards were such a well-liked and well-respected couple that it was hard to know where to begin in terms of who would have wanted Caroline Luard dead. Due to the high-profile nature of the case, Scotland Yard were quickly involved in the investigation, and two bloodhounds were deployed to the woods to see if the "disappointing footprints" which were found close to the body could lead the inquiry any further. There was a huge amount of interest in the role of the dogs, but unfortunately, despite following a number of trails several times, the scent led to a dead end once the dogs hit the main road.

The police efforts to search the bracken and gorse surrounding the summerhouse also produced disappointing results. The revolver wasn't found and the police were unable to establish what kind of gun was used as the bullets were smashed against the skull of the victim, making it impossible to form an accurate estimate of the calibre of the weapon. Police guarded the area around the crime scene while the investigation was carried out, but newspaper articles in the few days following the tragedy were able to confirm that there had been no disturbance at the summerhouse and that no break-in had been attempted. Meanwhile, Major-General Luard was so overcome with grief that he was very little help to the authorities; it was also clear that he had no idea who could have attacked his wife.

The inquest into the death of Caroline Luard was opened on 26th August 1908, in the dining room of Ightham Knoll, by Dr Buss, coroner for the Tonbridge division, Kent. Major-General Luard was the first witness called and gave his evidence in a low, firm voice. He confirmed the events of the afternoon Mrs Luard died, including the fact that when he saw his wife on the verandah of the summerhouse he at first thought she had suffered a fainting fit. He told the jury how his wife had been lying partly on her face, with her hat off. The pocket of her dress had been cut open. A brief examination led him to the conclusion that his wife was dead. His wife had also vomited close to where her body was found, suggesting that the blow to the head had made her sick. The killer then coldly shot the victim behind her right ear before firing for a second time into her left cheek. Major-General Luard confirmed at the inquest that he owned three revolvers but it was established by a leading expert that none of his guns had delivered the fateful shots to his wife. Two weeks after the initial inquest, proceedings were resumed at a local venue. In the meantime, Luard became the victim of a "whispering campaign", which suggested that he was the murderer. He even received anonymous letters accusing him of the crime. He was so distraught about the letters that he left Ightham Knoll, arranging to meet his eldest son, who was returning from South Africa where he was serving in the Army. However, before father and son could be reunited, Major-General Luard jumped in front of the 9.09am train from Maidstone West to Tonbridge.

Caroline Luard's inquest concluded with the verdict that the victim was "murdered by person or persons unknown". Major-General Luard was deduced to have committed suicide while suffering from temporary insanity. Although no killer was ever brought to justice, the police maintained that Caroline was murdered by someone known to her who had lain in wait for her. However, two years following her death, there was some speculation that her murderer was John Dickman, who was said to have borrowed money from Mrs Luard after she answered an advertisement he placed in *The Times*. There were rumours that Dickman had forged the amount on the cheque and that when Caroline Luard discovered his fraud she arranged to meet him without her husband's knowledge. Dickman was eventually tried and hanged for the murder of another victim – despite several attempts to gain him a reprieve – in 1910.

# Joseph Wilson

(1911)

On Saturday 7th October 1911, stationmaster Joseph Wilson had just seen off the last train for the night from Lintz Green station when sand was thrown in the eyes of the 60-year-old and he was shot dead.

The station was isolated – between Newcastle and Consett on the Derwent Valley line in County Durham – and police at first suspected robbery. However, the day's takings were left untouched. Situated a mile from the hamlet of Lintzford, the station was conveniently surrounded by trees and was ideally suited to be the scene of an isolated robbery. Wilson was a well-respected member of the community and staunch Methodist and it was a complete mystery to police why anyone would want to attack the quiet, elderly man.

Wilson did not die immediately, but was unable to give any insight into who had shot him or why. When the stationmaster died, it sparked one of the largest, most intensive murder investigations carried out in the northeast. There were no passengers waiting to catch the last train of the day, but waiting alongside Wilson were his colleagues, booking clerk Fred White and porter John Routledge. The latter got on the train, which would take him home, and four passengers left it, including Samuel Elliott, Charles Swinburne, Thomas Middleton and Robert Wailes. Swinburne was a friend of White and waited for the railway employee to finish his duties before the two headed towards home in Lintzford. Just as White was locking up the booking office, he and Swinburne heard a loud shot, which sounded as if it came not far from the stationmaster's house, just some 50 yards away. They ran towards the house, where Wilson's daughter, Bertha, was calling to them that her father had been shot. Elliott, Wailes and Middleton also heard the shot and came racing back to the station. The men carried the failing Wilson into his home where Middleton – a trained ambulanceman – tried to help. However, the stationmaster was covered in blood and unable to speak properly. He just "gurgled" in his last moments before his life ended abruptly. White returned to the booking office and telephoned for the police and a doctor. Within an hour, Superintendent Dryden from Consett and Dr Boland from Burnopfield arrived at the scene.

The following morning, the chief constable of Durham arrived to start an extensive investigation, while a post-mortem was carried out by Dr Boland, who confirmed that the stationmaster had been killed with a single gunshot wound from a revolver. Wilson's routine was well known and he usually took the takings home with him after the last train had left the station. However, on this particular Saturday, he had removed the takings earlier in the day. Once the investigation was under way, police found the bullet close to where the body had initially fallen, along with a small bag of sand, some linen cloth, and a number of footprints in the garden.

By the time the inquest began on the following Monday, more than 200 police officers were engaged in the murder hunt but, apart from the meagre clues left in and around Wilson's home, nothing else materialized.

The only suspect in the case was 25-year-old Samuel Atkinson, Lintz Green's relief porter, who was arrested on the Wednesday following the murder. Several witnesses confirmed that Atkinson had been hanging around the station long after his shift was over, although other witnesses were less sure. On this evidence he was accused of Wilson's murder, but his solicitor discovered that at no stage in proceedings had Atkinson been cautioned. He was remanded in custody for seven days by a magistrate and when he appeared before the court again, his solicitor once again brought up the issue of the caution. His previous statements could not be used in court due to the lack of a caution but he was remanded yet again until 9th November. Atkinson was put on trial for the murder of Joseph Wilson at the Assize Court in Durham but Durham chief constable William Morant could not bring any evidence against the young suspect. There were calls for Atkinson to be released and the case was duly dismissed. The police brought the investigation and prosecution to an abrupt end and Atkinson's guilt was neither proved or disproved. Despite a large, intense investigation, the murder of Joseph Wilson remains unsolved.

# Bella Wright

(Green Bicycle Case, 1919)

By the evening of Saturday 5th July 1919, Leicestershire police were hunting the murderer of 22-year-old Annie "Bella" Wright, who had been shot dead in the head with a heavy calibre revolver. The young farm labourer's daughter had left her home earlier that evening to cycle through the lanes and villages of the Fernie hunting country near Stoughton where she lived. She had called at the house of her uncle, George Measures, in Gaulby, where a male cyclist, on a green bicycle, appeared to be riding alongside her and had waited patiently outside for the young woman. When Wright left her relatives' home, the man cycled away with her in the direction of Stretton and Stoughton. Bella's dead body was found on the roadside of Gartree Road (or Via Devana) an hour or so later at around 9.20pm by a local farmer called Cowell. Despite police offering a reward for information leading to the arrest of the other cyclist, described as aged 35 to 45 and around five foot nine inches in height, the suspect and his green-enamelled BSA bicycle had simply disappeared.

Bella Wright was the oldest of seven children, and still lived with her parents in a cottage about two to three miles from Leicester. At the time of her murder she had a factory job at Bates Rubber Mill and she was known to be engaged to Archie Ward, a Royal Navy stoker. However, it came to light that Wright may also have had another suitor at the time. It was also established that the young woman possibly knew a man by the name of Ronald Vivian Light, a 34-year-old First World War veteran who not only owned a green bicycle but who later admitted – having denied it at first – that he had been cycling with the victim on the day she was killed.

Light was the only child of a successful inventor and had been expelled from Oakham School when he was 17 years old for supposedly lifting a young girl's clothes over her head. His reputation was further tainted by the fact that he had committed improper conduct with an 8-year-old girl and had tried to have a sexual relationship with a 15-year-old girl while in his early 30s. His criminal activities also extended to setting fire to haystacks while employed as a labourer on a farm, and setting fire to a cupboard and drawing indecent graffiti in a toilet when he was employed by the railway in 1914. His father committed suicide while Light was serving in the Army and his mother, in part, attributed her husband's death to their wayward son. When Light returned from serving as a gunner in the Honourable Artillery Company at the end of the First World War he was suffering from shell shock and was partially deaf.

Bella Wright met Light on the day she died at around 6.45pm, having asked the passing cyclist if he had a spanner she could borrow to fix the loose wheel on her bicycle. Although he didn't, he offered to accompany Wright to her uncle's cottage. When the couple rode away from the cottage in Gaulby, it was the last time that Bella Wright was seen alive. The police constable called to the scene was Alfred Hall; he was unconvinced by the doctor's explanation that the smears of blood on the top bar of a farmer's gate close to the body concluded that it was a simple accident. Dr Williams, from Billesdon, was sure that Wright had crashed her bike and was killed outright by a head injury. However, it was dark at the time and neither the policeman nor the doctor could see a great deal. Returning to the scene early the following day, Constable Hall found a bullet about 17 feet from the victim's body. While wiping her face, he discovered the bullet's entry wound – about an inch under her left eye – and the exit wound at the back of her skull. At the post-mortem, it was established that the bullet had been fired no more than four or five feet away from the victim.

For five months after the killing, Light hid his bicycle from view. He was then seen dismantling the bike and attempting to get rid of it in the River Soar over the Upperton Road Bridge in Leicester by labourer Samuel Holland. In late February 1920, the bicycle was found by Enoch Whitehouse, who was driving a horse-drawn boat of coal on the River Soar when the tow rope became snagged on its frame. Whitehouse immediately alerted police and, when they arrived at the scene, they discovered that the serial number and BSA emblem had been filed off the bike. However, a further serial number had not been filed quite enough and it was enough to link the bicycle to Light.

At the time of the discovery, Light was teaching maths at a school in Cheltenham, and it was here that he was arrested on 4th March 1920, by Detective Superintendent Taylor. According to Taylor, Light claimed he didn't have a bike, but that he had had a green bicycle which he "sold years ago". The suspect was then placed alongside nine other men and was identified by Henry Cox, the bike shop owner who had repaired Light's bicycle between 2nd July and 5th July 1919. Light was also identified by George Measures as the man who had been in his niece's company on the day of the murder. The suspect was remanded in custody prior to his trial at Leicester Castle on 23rd March 1920. Opening the case against Light was Director of Public Prosecutions, F J Sims. Evidence was heard from a number of witnesses, including Leicester gunsmith Henry Clark, who confirmed that the bullet which killed the victim was identical to those found in a gun holster which was dredged up with the bicycle from the canal. He went on to state that the cartridges were military issue and would not have been available to civilians. Light's earlier sexual exploits were never mentioned in court, although two young girls aged 12 and 14 were brought as witnesses to describe how, on the day of the attack, they had been chased by the suspect on their bicycles through country lanes. The prosecution also reconstructed the events leading to Wright's death and deduced that, about a mile west of leaving her uncle's house, the young woman had fled from Light. They believed that she panicked and headed south on a particularly narrow lane, which would have been a route home, although not the shortest. The prosecution concluded that Light had cut in front of the victim via a more direct route and lain in wait at the gate where the victim was shot dead. Light's defence came from Sir Edward Marshall Hall, who ensured that his questioning of witnesses was based more on technical issues. He also encouraged the suspect to admit to all events of the day of the murder, except the actual killing of the victim. Light, however, did admit to being the owner of a revolver. Marshall Hall argued that the fatal shot could have been accidental, which he thought likely, as a closer shot would undoubtedly have caused more damage to the victim's head. This, coupled with the fact that Light was well-spoken and had remained composed throughout the trial, managed to convince the jury that the mathematics master and former military man was not responsible for the death of the factory worker. After Light's acquittal, many theories, including accidental shooting, were raised, and two books on the murder came to completely different conclusions. As for Light, in 1928 he moved to the Isle of Sheppey, where he changed his name to Leonard Estelle and married an older woman. He died in 1975, leaving behind a stepdaughter who had no knowledge of his past life and his trial for murder until after his death at the age of 89. The case of who shot Bella Wright is still unsolved.

# Janet Smith

(1924)

In July 1924, wealthy socialites Frederick and Doreen Baker lived in the exclusive neighbourhood of Shaughnessy Heights, Vancouver, where their baby daughter, Rosemary, was cared for by Scottish nanny Janet Smith. Born in Perth, Scotland, in 1902, at the age of 11, Smith had moved to London with her parents, railway fireman Arthur Mitchell Tooner Smith and Joanna Smith (née Benzies). She began working for Baker, a prominent exporter of pharmaceuticals, and his wife in January 1923, and moved with the family three months later to Paris. In October that year, the Bakers moved back to their native Vancouver and Janet Smith went with them. Here she would remain until her untimely death at the age of 22. The Scottish nanny's death became one of Canada's most mysterious and unsolved crimes of the 20th century.

Also living in the house at the time of the murder was 25-year-old married man, and Chinese "houseboy", Wong Foon Sing, who was said to be infatuated with Smith. He often gave the Scottish nanny gifts and her friends reported at the time that she feared Wong. However, the case was "botched" by the Point Grey police who were called to the scene on 26th July 1924. Constable James Green was the first on the scene, where he found the dead victim; she had suffered a gunshot wound to the head from a .45 calibre revolver. The gun was lying a short distance from her body and the initial findings were that Smith had committed suicide. Wong gave a statement to police in which he said he had heard a noise like a car backfiring, but on investigation had found Smith's body lying in the basement of the house. Constable Green picked up the gun, which later made it impossible to identify any fingerprints. He further hampered the case when, despite the fact that the victim had been bashed on the back of the head, there were no powder burns to her face or hands, and no blood or brain tissue on the walls, he concluded that she had taken her own life. Of course, the lack of blood and brain tissue and the fact that there was no bullet found at the crime scene point to the victim having been shot from some distance.

At the inquest, the coroner concluded that the wound was self-inflicted and the death was recorded as accidental. The undertaker was then instructed to embalm the body – without a post-mortem being held – which led to all evidence on the victim's body being lost, and Smith was buried at Mountain View Cemetery. However, the undertaker did note at the time that there were suspicious unexplained burns on the right side of the body.

Dissatisfied with the verdict, the United Council of Scottish Societies, with input from Smith's friends, put pressure on the provincial government and Alexander Malcolm Manson, the attorney general, to reopen the case. It was to lead to a sensational case involving Vancouver's elite, which would expose widespread racism and political corruption. Wong Foon Sing was arrested and accused of Smith's murder despite the fact it became known that the victim had had an affair with her employer, Baker. She had also written many entries in her diary alluding to the fact that she liked being attractive to men and enjoyed their attentions. In August that same year, Smith's body was exhumed and a second inquest deduced that the victim had indeed been murdered. Matters were further stirred up by the gossip sheet *Vancouver Star*, which was quick to latch onto the scandals and sensationalism surrounding the case. Publisher Victor Odlum was hardly unbiased; one of his enemies of the time was General McRae, the father of Baker's sister-in-law. The prosecutor called to the case was Malcolm Jackson, who quickly identified Wong as the culprit because the houseboy was the only other occupant of the house – apart from the child – at the time of the murder. The *Vancouver Star* jumped on the bandwagon and pronounced Wong, in several articles, to be the likely perpetrator of the crime. As well as his hate for Baker, Odlum was anti-Asian and had made his distaste of whites and Asians being in close proximity very clear during the 1921 federal election. He even went so far as to publish an article on whether Chinese employees should be allowed to work alongside white girls, and called for legislation to bring about changes so that the two races were unable to mix, both personally and professionally.

Odlum was successful in his attempts and the Legislative Assembly introduced the Janet Smith Bill in November 1924, prohibiting employers from bringing Asian and white workers into the same household. However, with support from the *Vancouver Province*, which pointed out that the Bill violated Asian and Orientals' rights in accordance with the Anglo-Japanese Treaty of 1911, it failed at a second hearing. As a result, and with very little evidence – apart from his proximity to the victim at the time of the murder – Wong was released from custody and interest in the case gradually died down. But this wasn't the end of events for Wong, who was kidnapped by a group of men dressed as the Ku Klux Klan in March 1925. He was held captive and tortured for more than six weeks. Despite the atrocious circumstances in which he was held, Wong maintained his innocence and would not confess to the murder. He was eventually released in May 1925.

The case became even more sensational when it emerged that four policemen – including a detective sergeant, the chief of police and two police commissioners – were involved in the kidnapping of Wong, alongside three officials from the Scottish Societies. Three of the men admitted kidnap and torture and all were convicted; however, the jury made a recommendation of mercy. In a controversial move, the local government also barred prosecution of any of the men suspected of the houseboy's kidnap. The fact that Manson had known all along of Wong's whereabouts and who was holding him, yet did nothing to help the young man, was to severely damage the attorney general's professional reputation. Having been acquitted of murder, Wong returned to the employ of the Bakers but left Canada in 1926, bound for Hong Kong.

As with all unsolved crimes, the theories continued long after the case had come to a dead end. Baker was cited as the murderer in a book published 60 years after the nanny's death, while a story rife at the time was that Janet Smith was raped and murdered by a group of wealthy men who bribed the authorities to keep the incident quiet.

# Julia Wallace

(1931)

On Monday 19th January 1931, William Wallace arrived at the Liverpool Chess Club at the City Café to play a scheduled game. As he arrived at the club Wallace – an insurance agent with the Prudential – was handed a message, given over the telephone about 25 minutes earlier, requesting him to call the following evening at 7.30pm to discuss insurance with a Mr Qualtrough. The address stated in the message was 25 Menlove Gardens East. It would turn out to be bogus.

As a conscientious man, Wallace duly attempted to find the address the following night but, after searching for around 45 minutes – including asking passers-by, tram conductors, calling into a newsagent and stopping a policeman to make enquiries – he decided that his attempts were futile and made his way home. When Wallace reached his home in Wolverton Street, Anfield, he was unable to enter the house by either the front or the back door and mentioned this fact to Mr and Mrs Johnston, whom he met in the alley at the back of their houses. With the Johnstons as witnesses, he again tried the back door and this time it opened – to reveal his wife, Julia Wallace, lying battered to death in the sitting room. To begin with, detectives called to the scene were baffled by the murder. The assailant had left no clue and there were no signs of a struggle. However, one of the kitchen cabinet doors had been wrenched off and the cash box in which Wallace normally kept his insurance takings was empty of the little cash that had been kept there.

Wallace had only been away from home for about an hour and a half, during which time his wife had been murdered by a man, or men, who had gained entry without being seen or heard by neighbours on either side of the street. Wallace stated to police that he had never heard of a Mr Qualtrough and Chief Superintendent Moore of Liverpool CID did not suspect the victim's husband, who was often out collecting insurance money during the evenings. Apart from a small quantity of cash, nothing seemed to have been taken from the house. Police were astonished by bloodstains high up on the wall in the room where the murder was committed and the fact that there were none elsewhere in the room except on the piece of furniture against which Mrs Wallace lay dead. They were convinced that the murderer would have been badly bloodstained and the clothes likely to have been discarded. Via newspaper articles, they asked the public to let them know if any clothes like this were found in and around the city.

Despite the fact that the operator on the other end of the line who had taken the mysterious message for Wallace was adamant that the voice was not that of Julia's husband, as the telephone box used to convey the bogus message was just 400 feet from the Wallace's home the police began to suspect that William had murdered his wife after leaving himself the message to provide a concrete alibi. He was arrested two weeks after her death and questioned at length. Police also suspected that Wallace had murdered her prior to leaving his home for the 7.30pm meeting, and used a fit young detective to reconstruct the older man's movements on the night in question. However,

52-year-old Wallace was ailing and had had a kidney removed in 1907. The suit he was wearing on the night of the murder was examined but no evidence of blood was found; forensic examination of the crime scene concluded that the attack was so brutal and frenzied that the assailant would have been drenched in Julia Wallace's blood. There was also no evidence of blood in the bath or drains at the couple's home so the police theory that a naked Wallace had attacked his wife prior to going out also didn't fit. Wallace was steadfast in proclaiming his innocence. His trial was held at the Crown Court in Liverpool where the circumstantial evidence persuaded the jury in just over an hour of deliberations that Wallace was guilty of murder. He was sentenced to death. What was the most interesting aspect of the case, however, was the fact that the evidence was so flimsy that it could not categorically prove his guilt or innocence.

Despite the sentence, the jury's verdict was overturned by the Court of Criminal Appeal, which concluded that the evidence did not support the conviction. It was the first time in British legal history that a jury was found to be wrong. Wallace lived out the remainder of his short life on the Wirral after retiring from insurance due to ill health. He died in 1933, just two years after his wife.

Further investigations, long after Wallace's trial, by crime writer Jonathan Goodman and radio news editor Roger Wilkes, both point to a man that worked with Wallace at the Prudential. The man was well known to Julia Wallace and she would have been likely to let him into the house. Twenty-two-year-old Richard Gordon Parry was a petty criminal who worked as a junior within Wallace's firm. He used his former girlfriend to falsify an alibi for him at the time of the murder which, coupled with a bloody glove found near his car on the night in question, gave rise to a much stronger case against him than against Wallace. It is possible that police did suspect Parry at the time, but the lack of evidence and the fact that the public were outraged at the killing prompted police to wrongly arrest Wallace. Parry died in 1980 without admitting to the crime but, as evidence was uncovered, it was found that he had a detailed knowledge of the crime and that of the deaths of several witnesses who were originally connected to the case.

The murder of Julia Wallace is still officially unsolved.

# Sir Harry Oakes

(1943)

"Son-in-law accused of murder for gain" was the headline of the *Daily Mirror* on 19th October 1943 – it referred to the case of Alfred de Marigny, who pleaded not guilty to the murder of his wealthy father-in-law, Sir Harry Oakes. Sir Harry, who was 68, was found dead at his home in Nassau on 9th July that same year. Cambridge University graduate Adderley opened the case for the prosecution, where he gave three reasons for the murder: "revenge, satisfaction and gain". He told the jury that de Marigny had delivered four blows to Sir Harry's head and that: "any of them would have killed ... but the murderer was so filled with hate and malice that he struck again and again, and then burned the body".

Sir Harry's story was ultimately a tragic one. He had been a young man who was determined to realize his dreams of becoming rich. He abandoned his medical career to seek his fortune in gold and he ventured from his home in the US to the Klondike where he was shipwrecked off the Alaskan coast and taken prisoner by the Russians. He faced freezing to death on two occasions in Alaska before finally making his way to Kirkland Lake, Ontario, Canada. With financial backing from his mother, it was here that Oakes made his fortune, when his daring decision to mine beneath the lake paid off, making him a reported $60,000 a day. Oakes was generous with his wealth and gave shares to friends – particularly those who had helped him –

and family, making each of them extremely rich in the process. While taking a world cruise, he met and married Australian Eunice MacIntyre, who was 20 years his junior, in June 1923. The couple had five children and eventually settled on the island of Nassau in the Bahamas. Here, Oakes was renowned for his generosity and philanthropic attitude to life as he set about tackling the island's poverty by employing many locals in his quest to build his empire on Nassau; he also provided a transport system and hospital wing for locals. It came as a huge shock to the islanders when it was discovered that Oakes was murdered in a possible sadistic ritual. His body was discovered by close friend Harold Christie, who was staying the night at Sir Harry's Westbourne home and who had twice been woken in the night by mosquitoes and a thunderstorm. Christie told the inquest that: "I went to the screen door and called 'Hi Harry'. There was no answer. I opened the door, I saw the burned mosquito bar with the net missing, and rushed to the bed and lifted Harry's head." The body had been saturated in petrol and set alight while a Chinese screen close to the bed was found to be covered in blood and smudged handprints. Hidden by the blood covering the dead man's face and head were the four blows to the head as described by Adderley.

The trial of Sir Harry's son-in-law, Alfred de Marigny, came about when the Duke of Windsor and Governor of the Bahamas – formerly King Edward VIII – took over the case because he was a close friend of Oakes. However, the duke was absent from the Bahamas during the trial so as to avoid being called as a witness. Despite attempts to censor the press, the case drew worldwide interest because of who the victim was and the grisly nature in which he died. However, the Second World War raging across the globe made it difficult to proceed and two US policemen were drafted in to conduct the investigation instead of Scotland Yard. De Marigny had eloped with Oakes' daughter Nancy to New York in 1942, just two days after her 18th birthday. De Marigny, a competitive sailor, had met Nancy at the Nassau Yacht Club two years earlier and had managed to keep the seriousness of their relationship a secret until after their wedding. De Marigny had been married twice before to wealthy women and was known to have led a playboy lifestyle. It is hardly surprising that Sir Harry was less than enamoured with his son-in-law, who was 16 years older than his daughter. Witnesses would testify to the fact that the two men did not get on and had had rows on several occasions. The Oakes family were all away at the time of the murder and, when Nancy learned of her father's death, she travelled to the family's summer home in Maine to join her mother. But, convinced of her husband's innocence, she returned to Nassau in order to organize his defence by bringing in private investigators Raymond Schindler and Godfrey W Higgs. However, she was alone in her quest, with many of her family members believing de Marigny guilty of the crime of which he was accused.

On the night of the murder, de Marigny had hosted his own dinner party that finished in the early hours of the following morning. The chief evidence against him was a fingerprint found on the Chinese screen close to Sir Harry's half-burned body, but it was later found that the print had actually come from a glass that de Marigny had drunk from while being questioned by the US police. Sir Harry's son-in-law came close to being hanged for the offence but the lack of evidence against him saw him acquitted, especially when it was suspected that the police had fabricated it. Many thought that de Marigny was being framed and, under further investigation, the professionalism and techniques used by leading policeman Captain Baker were called into question. Furthermore, de Marigny testified at his own trial that he hadn't been near Westbourne for more than two years, following disagreements between the family. This was partly backed by Lady Eunice Oakes who confirmed, in a tearful testimony at the trial, that she had made: "Many attempts at reconciliation with Nancy, and finally received a letter from her saying she and her husband would have nothing to do with the family 'until Alfred is received into the family circle'." De Marigny was further helped by his dinner guests, one of whom was in a car being driven home by his host at the time of the murder. Nancy de Marigny possibly also helped her husband's case. Beautiful and vivacious, the young woman was popular with the press and continued to maintain her husband's innocence in the death of her father. Sir Harry's murderer was never brought to justice and the case remains unsolved.

# Charles Walton

(1945)

Was witchcraft to blame for the death of 74-year-old widower Charles Walton on 14th February 1945? Walton, an agricultural worker and farm labourer, had lived in the vicinity of Lower Quinton, Warwickshire, all his life. He'd adopted his niece Edith "Edie" Walton upon the death of her mother some 30 years earlier, and she still lived with him at 15 Lower Quinton, which they rented for three shillings a week. Well-liked, although considered eccentric by some, Walton was a loner who, at his time in life, relied upon a stick for walking due to his rheumatic joints. On the day he died, Charles Walton was seen by two witnesses at around 9.00am passing through the churchyard on his way to work at a local farm, The Firs, for farmer Alfred Potter.

According to local reports, Walton was carrying his own tools, including a hayfork and a trouncing hook. Despite his age and infirmness, the agricultural hand still liked to take light work where he could and had been working as a casual labourer for Potter for the past nine months. He was due to cut hedges in a field on Meon Hill, known as Hillground. He was a true country man, and today would undoubtedly have been known as an animal whisperer due to his ability to tame wild dogs just by using his voice, and to attract the birds that flocked to him. Walton was a creature of habit and was due home at around 4.00pm so, when his niece returned home at 6.00pm and found that he hadn't arrived back, she was worried. Walton had no real friends as such and was not known for visiting the local pub or other people's houses. However, Warwickshire is renowned for its deep associations with witchcraft and it was widely accepted that Walton had various connections to covens operating in the area at the time. Edie immediately asked their neighbour, Harry Beasley, to accompany her on the walk up to The Firs. Potter hadn't seen Walton to speak to, but earlier that day he had seen in the distance a lone figure cutting hedges whom he assumed was the elderly man. The three of them decided to make their way to where Walton had last been seen. The night had by this time drawn in, so the small party carried torches, enabling them to quickly find Walton's dead body.

He had been murdered with his own trouncing hook, which lay embedded in his throat, while his body had been pinned to the ground with the pitchfork. He had a large cross carved into his chest. The grisly murder was to spark a major police investigation, which began immediately. Walton's mutilated body was carried down the hillside to the village where Superintendent Alec Spooner of the local CID began investigating the crime. However, Scotland Yard, headed up by Detective Superintendent Robert Fabian, was called in within a few days, such was the public outcry at the macabre death. Sergeant Webb, who accompanied Fabian from London, was convinced that the murderer was a lunatic, however Spooner – who was still part of the investigation – suggested something far more sinister. The local policeman was quick to point out that the case had similarities to that of Ann Turner, who had been stabbed with a pitchfork in 1875 by the local "village idiot" because he thought the woman had bewitched him and the local farmland. He backed his suspicions with evidence from a book written by Revd James Harvey Bloom in 1929 entitled *Folklore, Old Customs and Superstitions in Shakespeare Land*. Suspicions rose further when it was discovered that the book mentioned a farm lad named Charles Walton, who had seen a large black dog on several days on his way to work. The police were convinced at the time that the book was talking of the same Charles Walton. It was evident from the victim's body that he had been killed in the same way in which witches had been slain – by a method known as "sticking" – in Anglo-Saxon times, when it was believed this was the only way to stop a dead witch from rising from the grave. But, despite the evidence and the similarities in the cases, Fabian and Webb felt huge public pressure to close the case as quickly as possible. Air and ground searches revealed nothing of much help to the police and Walton's pocket watch, which was missing from the body, was not traced. All the villagers were interviewed by the team from Scotland Yard and a huge map in the investigation room showed where each and every one of the inhabitants said they were at the time of the murder. An Italian prisoner of war was detained a few days later, but was released when it was discovered he had only done some poaching in the area to supplement his meagre diet.

Meanwhile, the post-mortem carried out on Walton revealed he had been hit over the head with his own walking stick, that his trachea had been cut, and that the injuries to his chest had broken several ribs. Defensive wounds were also found on the victim's hands and forearms. As the last person to have seen Walton alive, suspicion soon fell on Farmer Potter, who claimed that he had seen the victim, in his shirtsleeves, working along the hedges of his field at around 2.00pm on the day he was killed. But, although interviewed twice, there was nothing else on which the police could rely in order to seriously suspect Alfred Potter. However, as the police did establish that the victim had not actually been in shirtsleeves at the time of the crime because the he was wearing a jacket when found, did Potter see the murderer?

As Fabian's 20th-century murderer simply didn't seem to exist, the hardened Londoner returned reluctantly to the witchcraft theory still strongly supported by Spooner. It seemed that Walton had possibly been murdered as a blood sacrifice in order to ensure a good harvest that year. But villagers remained mute on the subject and refused to talk to the police about pagan rituals. The police investigation then decided to focus on Walton's past in an effort to see whether foul play had come about because of any prior incidents. They discovered that Walton's bank account was pretty empty, despite the fact that he'd been left almost £300 by his wife in 1927. Apart from the strange disappearance of the money – Walton was a frugal man who had worked all his life – they found nothing. With nothing to go on, and no real motive for the killing, the Scotland Yard detectives returned to London and the inquest recorded Walton's death as "murder by person or persons unknown".

However, Spooner was reluctant to let the case go and continued a personal campaign to find the murderer, whom he suspected was a local. Even many years after his retirement, Spooner was known to have revisited the spot where Walton died on the anniversary of the murder. Walton's pocket watch, which went missing from the murder scene, was eventually discovered in 1960 behind some outhouses close to the elderly man's cottage. As the police had searched the area in 1945 and found nothing, it is assumed that the murderer returned some time later to dispose of the watch near Walton's home.

# Betty Short

(The Black Dahlia, 1947)

In newspaper reports in late January 1947, an article describing the arrest of Edward Thorpe, read: "Falling asleep in a Hollywood bus, Edward Thorpe, 35, babbled: 'I forgot to cut the scar off her leg' – and was arrested for the murder of Betty Short, film city play-girl, whose mutilated body was found in a field four days ago. Betty, known as the Black Dahlia because of her raven hair and fondness for clinging black dresses, had dozens of sweethearts. She was last seen driving with a handsome ex-marine known as 'Red'. Police believe that the killer tortured Betty before strangling her and cutting her body in half. Thorpe, whose bus-babbling was told to the police by fellow passengers, had stains on his clothing resembling blood." However, like others in this case, Thorpe's arrest came to nothing.

Elizabeth "Betty" Short had become the victim of a gruesome and high-profile murder. She went missing on 9th January 1947 and wasn't seen again until her body was discovered. Known as Betty as a child, Elizabeth preferred to be called Beth as she grew up. Born in Boston, Massachusetts, in 1924, Betty was only five years old when her father, Cleo Short, went missing in 1929; it was suspected he had committed suicide. He later wrote to Short's mother Phoebe, apologizing for leaving and asking if he could return, but his wife refused. Meanwhile, for Beth, movies were her life and she was desperate to work on screen. She moved to Vallejo, California, for a time, before moving to Los Angeles with her father. The pair fell out and Beth then moved to Santa Barbara before returning to Hollywood where she was determined to make her name. On 15th January 1947, her severely mutilated body was found in the Crenshaw district. However, following the discovery of the young woman's body, the lack of evidence would hamper the investigation and leave the case of "The Black Dahlia" – as Short was nicknamed by the press – as one of Hollywood's enduring unsolved crimes.

Despite a genital defect which left Short unable to have sexual intercourse in the usual way, she was beautiful, vivacious and outgoing. She liked the attention of men and there were copious rumours about why the wannabe actress was murdered. With her aspiration to be famous and her renowned love of servicemen, Short was a different kind of woman, not afraid to be seen and heard while keeping company with various men and women. There was even a rumour that she had close connections to Marilyn Monroe for a time.

Short's naked, mutilated body was spotted by a passer-by in a field; it was bruised, beaten and cut in half. It seemed that grass had been forced into her vagina and that she had also reportedly been sodomized following death. In addition, her face had been slashed from the corners of her mouth towards her ears, gruesomely distorting the young woman's features. The body had also been washed and cleaned and then, once dumped, had been posed with the hands over the head and elbows bent. Once the news of Short's death was released to the press, a number of men and women admitted to the crime, but police were unable to verify whether any of those who came forward were actually involved or not. For some reason, it seemed that the death of "the Black Dahlia" would bring about many – perhaps as many as 50 – false confessions. One woman confessed to the killing because Short had stolen her boyfriend. She was unable to give the police any details of the crime and later admitted she made the story up. There were many stories like this, but those that seemed more plausible – yet were subsequently untrue – resulted in the suspect being sent into psychiatric care. One man was even detained in a mental institution for his false confession. What was fairly shocking at the time was why anyone would want to be charged for a crime they didn't commit. However, the murder had been completely sensationalized by the press and the case had reached far and wide across the globe. Those in authority believed that the false confessions mainly came about as a way to gain fame and notoriety.

The fact that Short was cut in two sparked great interest in the case. There were those that claimed a butcher's knife had been used, while others were convinced that the body had been cut with precision and care with a saw or medical instrument. There were even claims at the time that the victim was alive – if unconscious – at the time she was dismembered and that her limbs were held down in some way. Her body was also clearly drained of blood before being dumped in the field in Crenshaw.

At the post-mortem, it was discovered that Short had marks on her wrists and ankles that were probably made by rope with which she had either been tied up or hung upside down. The victim had also suffered a number of blows to the head and the cause of death was found to be blood loss from the lacerations to her face and shock due to concussion. As the case continued, the coverage in the press became increasingly outrageous, with claims that Short's lifestyle had made her "victim" material. However, those that knew the wannabe actress were adamant that Short lived a fairly clean and healthy life despite her attraction to both sexes. Following a package that was delivered to the *Los Angeles Examiner* in late January with an address book inside with the name Mark Hansen embossed on the cover, the man himself – known to have been the last person to see Short alive – quickly became the prime suspect. Someone claiming to be the killer had already phoned the newspaper to say that items belonging to the victim could be sent if the paper needed motivation to keep the story "alive", and alongside the address book were Short's birth certificate and business cards. The "killer" kept writing to the newspaper, calling himself the "Black Dahlia Avenger". However, the Los Angeles police were convinced that their case was being hampered by the local media who were quick to sensationalize any new piece of evidence that came to light, as well as withholding vital information and trampling over the crime scene. Reporters were also spending time at the police station and were even known to have answered phones. Crucial tip-offs were never passed on to the police, who had to read about them in the press the following day once the reporter who answered the telephone had got their "scoop". The police didn't have any real evidence against Hansen.

Sometime later, the parallels between "The Black Dahlia's" case and that of mutilated six-year-old Suzanne Degnan (in Chicago) in 1946 were brought to light, and it was discovered that the writing of the Degnan ransom note and that of the person writing to the Los Angeles press was strikingly similar, with a combination of capitals and lower case letters. William Heirens was convicted of Suzanne Degnan's murder, but he has always maintained his innocence.

# The Somerton Man

(1948)

Interest in the case of an unidentified man found dead on Somerton beach in Adelaide, Australia, on 1st December 1948 was heightened and sparked much speculation due to the Cold War, which began roughly two years before the victim's death. The man, who has never been formally identified, was poisoned with an unknown substance, and the case remains one of Australia's most notorious unsolved ones. The man was found wearing a suit – but no hat, which was unusual in 1948 – and all the labels on his clothes had been removed. His clothing was obviously of good quality and included a white shirt, striped tie, brown trousers, a brown knitted pullover, a grey and brown double-breasted coat (although the weather in Australia in December is hot), socks and shoes. The victim was also clean-shaven with no distinguishing marks, and no identification was found on his body. At around five feet, 11 inches tall, the man was presumed to be around 40 to 45 years old with fair to red-coloured hair and hazel eyes. His hands showed no signs of manual labour while his calf muscles were pronounced like those of a ballet dancer or runner. The police were prone to believe that the man had committed suicide, although dental records showed that he didn't match any missing persons. What the police did find was an unsmoked and a half-smoked cigarette, some juicy fruit chewing gum, a bus ticket, rail ticket (unused) and an American comb, and some cigarettes sold exclusively in Britain along with some Bryant & May matches.

Witnesses claimed to have seen a man fitting the description of the victim around 7.00pm the night before. Another couple claimed to have seen the man a little later than this on the beach, unmoving, despite the mosquitoes around. They didn't investigate because they believed the man to be asleep or drunk, and were convinced that in the half an hour that he was in their view he had changed his position, although neither of them saw him move. When the body was discovered at around 6.30am the following morning, it was in the same position as that described by witnesses the night before, with the left arm straight and the right arm bent. The post-mortem revealed that the man died around 2.00am on 1st December; so it is possible that the man was alive when seen by witnesses between 8.00pm and 8.30pm the previous evening. It also revealed that much of the body was congested and the pathologist Dr Dwyer, despite finding nothing to suggest otherwise, was convinced the man did not die of natural causes. Dr Dwyer was sure that the man had been poisoned by a barbiturate or soluble hypnotic. However, he was unable to reach a conclusion as to the cause of death, the man's identity or the source of the poison, which was not believed to have been in the last meal he had eaten, around three or four hours prior to death. The man's photograph and fingerprints were circulated across the globe but no identification was made as to whom he was or where he had come from. As the man remained unknown, the body was embalmed just 10 days after his death.

For a short time, some Australian media believed the identity of the man to be E C Johnson but, after the missing man walked into a police station and declared himself to be "alive and well", a picture of the dead man was published in *The News*. Despite several calls from the public, the man remained unidentified and South Australian police confirmed that the victim's fingerprints were not held on record. Robert Walsh was also a missing man who had left Adelaide to buy sheep in Queensland several months earlier. The body of the man was identified by three separate witnesses as that of Robert Walsh but, at 63, he was thought too old to be the dead man. A former witness who stated that it was Robert Walsh, retracted her statement following a second viewing of the body and believed that the man was not the woodcutter from Adelaide. Several other identifications were also made of the man but police were unconvinced by witnesses' claims and stated that the only real evidence to the man's identity was the clothes he wore.

A breakthrough seemed possible in January 1949 when a brown suitcase was found at the railway station in Adelaide. Crucially, an orange waxed thread (not found in Australia) was discovered in the case, which turned out to be the same thread that had been used to mend the trousers the dead man had been wearing. In the case were items with the name T Keane, or Keane, but the police were still not convinced that this was the victim's name. T Keane was traced to a Tom Keane, a sailor who was also missing at the time; however, shipmates of Tom were adamant that the body in the morgue was not that of their former colleague.

The initial inquest began just a few days after the dead man was discovered on the beach, but was adjourned until June 1949. The investigating pathologist, Sir John Burton Cleland, re-examined the body and found that the man's shoes were exceptionally well-polished, which led him to believe that the unidentified victim had been dumped at Somerton beach – rather than walking around all day as previously thought – and backed this theory with the lack of vomiting and evidence of convulsions that were absent from the scene, and probably would not have been had the man been poisoned and left to die where he was later found. However, the pathologist was also keen to point out that this was merely speculation, as witnesses who had seen the man on the beach the night of 30th November were convinced the same man had been found dead the following morning. He concluded that there was no evidence as to the man's identity. However, a tiny piece of rolled-up paper with the words "Tamam Shud" was found deep in a fob pocket sewn within the trouser pocket of the dead man. Experts deduced that the words meant "ended" or "finished" from a collection of poems called *The Rubaiyat of Omar Khayyam*. This vital evidence was released to the public and brought about a surprising turn of events.

A man – whose identity was concealed at the time – discovered a rare first edition copy of a translation of the book by Edward Fitzgerald on the back seat of his unlocked car in Glenelg, where the man was found, on the day of the murder. The man, who was later revealed to be a doctor, did not connect the two incidents until he read about the poems in the newspaper. The poem's subject – which was to live a full life and not be disappointed when death arrived – led the police to believe the victim had committed suicide. The doctor's rare edition of the poems was missing the words "Tamam Shud" on the last page. Following further information about a man named Alfred Boxall, who came later into the police investigations, it was suggested that the dead man was a Soviet spy poisoned by his enemies, especially as his body was found in Adelaide, close to Woomera, which was known to be a secret missile launching and intelligence site during the Cold War. The man was eventually buried on 14th June 1949 by the Salvation Army in a funeral service that was paid for by the South Australian Grandstand Bookmakers Association. The case is still considered "open" by the South Australian Major Crime Task Force.

# Emily Armstrong

(1949)

Emily Armstrong (born around 1880) was beaten to death on 14<sup>th</sup> April 1949, and was found at a dry cleaner's shop on St John's Wood High Street, London, where she worked. Her body was found at around 4.00pm and police forensics showed she had been murdered about an hour before the grisly discovery was made. The victim, who lived with her son and daughter-in-law in Mountbell Road, Stanmore, Middlesex, was found – during the post-mortem – to have suffered more than 22 blows from a blunt object to her skull, which had been shattered by the force of the attack. The pathologist later declared that the instrument that killed Armstrong was a claw hammer.

To those passing by the dry cleaners on the high street, nothing appeared to be out of the ordinary. In fact, all seemed quite normal. The torn piece of paper stuck to the glass door on that Thursday afternoon read: "Closed – open Saturday". However, customers awaiting their dry-cleaned outfits for the Easter weekend banged and rattled the shop door, through which they could see the clothes they had dropped off earlier in the week for manager Armstrong to clean. Customers could also see a woollen dress, in two shades of blue, on the counter, where Mrs Armstrong had put it down for a moment, and the order book, lying open, next to the dress. The alarm was raised and police cars were soon screeching to a halt outside the shop on the high street. Detectives from Scotland Yard literally filled the tiny shop and those that stayed around to see what was happening witnessed the battered body of 69-year-old Armstrong being taken away by ambulance.

Police then began to interview witnesses, who claimed that when Mrs Armstrong had had lunch at the Marigold Café further down the high street, she mentioned that she had had to chase a strange man out of the shop's backyard earlier that morning. Two days after the murder, police were still, according to newspaper reports, trying to trace the man, the murderer and the weapon used to kill Mrs Armstrong. The police were also wondering whether the killer was the same man that had killed another lady, elderly Kathleen Higgins, a few weeks earlier. Seventy-five-year-old Higgins had been found murdered in the ground of Wingfield House, about 100 yards away from Armstrong's shop. In the case of Emily Armstrong, the police were satisfied that one of the motives for the attack was robbery, as the till had been emptied on the day of her murder and the victim's handbag was missing. But, as the shop would have contained little money, the police were known to suspect that the attack was also motivated by other reasons.

Armstrong's handbag was found quite close to the scene of the murder, together with a bloody handkerchief. This bore a laundry mark on it, but as a piece of evidence it did not prove helpful in the overall investigation. Witnesses described a man in his early 30s, who was seen in the vicinity of the murder, but police were unable to identify him. A murderer that had escaped from Broadmoor Hospital was also recaptured and paraded in a line-up, but witnesses were unable to identify him as the suspect seen close to the shop around the time of the murder. Several people were questioned in the investigation, but all were eventually released. Police were unable to get any further with the case and it remains unsolved today.

# The Boy in the Box

(1957)

The Vidocq Society, so named after the 18th-century French detective François Vidocq, is based in Philadelphia in the United States. The society dedicates itself, just as their namesake did, to solving unsolved or "cold" case deaths. Cases are officially brought to this exclusive organization in an attempt to find out what happened to victims of serious crimes that have so far eluded the authorities. One of the most significant cases that the society is dedicated to solving is that of the "Boy in the Box" also known as "America's Unknown Child".

The case began on 25th February 1957 on a narrow country lane in the Fox Chase area of northeast Philadelphia. Susquehanna Road was wooded to the south at the time and opened out onto open fields and scrubland. It was not a residential area, although to the north of the road was the commune of the Sister of the Good Shepherd, a religious order which aimed to help troubled young girls. Just opposite the driveway to the commune, the "Boy in the Box" was found in a thicket, naked, wrapped in a blanket, and face up in a large cardboard box. The small child was aged between four and six years old. He had been found several days earlier by a local man checking his traps, which were set in the vicinity of the body; however, fearing contact with the police, the man was reluctant to come forward about discovering the body. A college student stumbled across the young child's body a few days later and reported the incident to the police the following day.

The boy's hands had been folded across his stomach and he was clean, with recently cut finger and toenails. His hair had also been cut in what looked to be a haphazard way, either just prior to death or soon afterwards, and clumps of hair still clung to the boy's body. With blue eyes, fair to light-brown hair and pale skin, the victim appeared malnourished (and he certainly hadn't eaten for at least three hours prior to death). There was nothing in the box that could identify who he was or where he had come from. The eyes showed evidence of a serious eye condition, which had been treated to some extent. The child had seven scars on his tiny body and he was covered in bruises. Three of the scars – around the chest and groin – could possibly have been as the result of surgical procedures. In addition, there was a scar on the boy's left ankle, which could have related to the victim having been given an infusion or transfusion. The right hand and soles of his feet were "wrinkled", suggesting that either before or soon after death, they had been submerged in water for a long time. The weather was cold in Philadelphia in February 1957 and it was impossible to tell how long the boy had been dead, but it could have been between three days and a fortnight. Death occurred due to the head injuries the boy had suffered.

Someone had given birth to this child, someone had raised him and someone had killed him. Someone had to know who he was. No one reported the child missing and no one ever came forward to claim him. However, when the police released their official poster of the child on 8th March 1957, they were confident that it wouldn't be long before someone came forward with information that would solve the case and enable them to put the "Boy in the Box" to rest. But they were wrong.

Extensive resources and effort – including 270 police trainees and 50 police officers – were drafted in by police commissioner Thomas J Gibbons in the search for evidence and clues as to the boy's identity and the events surrounding his tragic death. But, despite the blanket, cardboard box and a man's cap found 17 feet from the box, there was very little for the police to go on. The box itself was one of 12, which had originally been sold as the container for a baby's bassinet sold by the J C Penney Co between March 1956 and February 1957. The shop had a "cash only" policy, which made it difficult to identify the 12 customers who had bought the bassinet. However, 11 were eventually traced and found to have no connection to the case. The box in which the boy was found appeared to have a white colouring inside it, suggesting that the bassinet in that particular box was white. Despite work carried out by the FBI lab, nothing further was discovered about the box and no clear fingerprints were detected. The royal blue corduroy cap that was found close to the scene was included on the original poster campaign to try and jog someone's memory. It still contained the tissue paper that the manufacturer had inserted in order to preserve its shape. Hannah Robbins, owner of the hat company that made the cap, confirmed that it was one of 12 caps made by the firm, but that this particular cap had been bought by a man who requested that a strap and buckle be sewn onto the back. Mrs Robbins was confident that the man who had bought the cap resembled the dead child; however, the cap yielded no further clues despite the best efforts of the FBI. She described the man as in his late 20s with fair hair and no accent. A man's white handkerchief found close to the crime scene also gave no clues, despite the initial "G" in one corner.

The blanket in which the child was wrapped also offered little for the police to go on. It was clean, made of cotton flannel, with a plaid design of diamonds and blocks in brown, green, rust and white, and had been cut in half. But this was a common design that had sold in its thousands from wholesalers across the country. A child's scarf and yellow flannel shirt – which would have fitted the victim – were also found close by, along with a pair of black children's shoes (size 1), although these did not fit the child. Nothing significant was picked up at the boy's post-mortem, although fingerprints and footprints were taken to compare with hospital and birth records. These also yielded nothing.

Over time, many theories were applied to the case, but two in particular were seriously investigated by the police and other authorities in the years that followed. A local investigator in the medical examiner's office, Remington Bristow, spent more than 36 years on the case, often on his own time and using his own money. He first became involved after contacting a New Jersey psychic who persuaded him to look for a house that was similar to a foster home, which was about one and a half miles from where the boy's body was found. The psychic then travelled to Philadelphia and led the investigator straight to the house where a bassinet, similar to those sold by J C Penney, and blankets, were found. The man running the foster home had a stepdaughter who, Bristow was convinced, was the boy's mother. Despite the abuse and neglect that the boy had suffered, he determined that the child had died accidentally but that, fearing her unmarried status, the woman had panicked and dumped the child rather than face the stigma of her situation. However, no concrete links were found between the woman and the boy, and DNA testing years later ruled the woman out as the boy's mother. The child's body was exhumed in 1998 by the FBI in order to gather tissue samples for DNA analysis and eventually an independent laboratory extracted samples from the boy's teeth.

A second, more recent, theory came from a woman identified as "M" in February 2002, some 45 years after the "Boy in the Box" case was opened. The woman claimed that her abusive mother had bought the child from his birth parents and that he suffered physical and sexual abuse at the hands of his "owner" until she killed him in a frenzied attack by banging his head on the floor after he had vomited in the bath. The story could well have been true, but former neighbours of "M" were adamant that there had never been a boy in the house, and as the woman had a history of mental illness, the theory was not pursued further.

Despite the passing of time, the Vidocq Society continues in their quest to find the truth behind the tragic story of the unknown child.

# Wendy Sewell

(1973)

Witness Charles Carman saw typist Wendy Sewell enter Bakewell Cemetery at around 12.50pm on 12th September 1973. Shortly after, 32-year-old Sewell was savagely attacked and left for dead. The victim had been beaten around the head with a pickaxe handle and sexually assaulted; her shoes, trousers and parts of her underwear had been removed. Sewell died two days later at the Chesterfield Royal Hospital without identifying her attacker. By the middle of February the following year, newspaper reports read: "Her killer was 17-year-old Stephen Downing, who worked in the cemetery, it was alleged at Nottingham Crown Court." Despite maintaining his innocence, Downing, who was a cemetery groundskeeper with a reading age of 11, became the primary suspect. He was questioned by police for nine hours without a solicitor present, during which time he reported that the reason he had the victim's blood on his clothes was because he had found her covered in blood and she shook her head while she lay on the ground. Downing eventually signed a confession – which, it was alleged later, the police had written for him – although he pleaded not guilty during his trial on 13th to 15th February 1974. Giving expert medical evidence, forensic scientist Norman Lee claimed at the trial that Downing could only have been covered in the victim's blood if he had committed the attack. At the time, Downing had admitted to sexually assaulting Sewell as she lay in the cemetery; however, he later denied this.

The jury convicted the 17-year-old of murder, unaware that he had a limited mental capacity, and he was sentenced to an indefinite period in prison, with the judge stipulating that he should serve a minimum of 10 years. As Downing maintained his innocence, he was ineligible to apply for parole.

Downing had the backing of his family, who were committed to proving their son's innocence. His parents, Ray and Juanita Downing, were quoted as saying: "We just want him home." The young cemetery worker had been seen leaving the cemetery before the attack took place by a female witness. As she also confirmed that she had seen Sewell unharmed after Downing left, he then applied to appeal his sentence on the testimony of the new witness. The Court of Appeal heard the grounds for appeal on 25th October 1974, but decided that the witness's evidence was unreliable, as any view of Sewell walking towards the back of the chapel would have been obstructed by trees. The appeal was denied. More than 27 years later, Downing made the newspapers again when, at the age of 44 in November 2000, new evidence suggested that the conviction was unsafe and that he would soon be released on bail. Both Downing and his parents were said to be "delighted" and "overjoyed" at the decision by the Criminal Cases Review Commission to take his conviction to the Court of Appeal. In addition, the police were accused of 17 separate mistakes, made at the outset of the case. However, the witness (who was 15 years old at the time of the original application for appeal) was found to be short-sighted and deemed unreliable.

But, there were others who had been campaigning for Downing's release alongside his family for several years, including Don Hale, editor of the *Matlock Mercury*. During the campaign, Downing protested his innocence while Sewell's character and promiscuity was called into question. It was known that Wendy Sewell had several secret lovers at the time and the case was dubbed "The Bakewell Tart". But, in December 2000, a judge ruled that Downing should not be granted his freedom, and opposed bail on the grounds that he had not had enough time to read the case papers. The news was met with fury by those campaigning for Downing's release, including MP for West Derby, Patrick McLoughlin, who said: "This is ludicrous. I am so angry at the injustice." Don Hale also commented at the time, saying he was: "gutted by the decision … I just cannot believe it". Prosecutors were blamed for not passing on the papers in time and Downing was faced with spending his 28th Christmas in jail for a crime he was adamant he didn't commit. Downing was said to be very depressed at having to remain in Littlehey prison in Cambridgeshire.

Two months later, in February 2001, Downing was freed, having spent 27 years behind bars for the murder he vehemently denied committing. The Court of Appeal heard on 7th February 2001 that both the prosecution and defence now accepted that Downing's original confession should have been ruled inadmissible. The hearing took 40 minutes and Mr Justice Pitchford granted bail, pending a full appeal hearing within three months. The Crown didn't oppose bail and conceded that the appeal was highly likely to succeed. The decision was faxed to Littlehey prison and Downing was released at 4.10pm. He celebrated with his parents, Ray and Juanita, and his sister Caroline at a local restaurant, before returning to the family home for the first time in 27 years. More than 13,000 locals had signed a petition for his release, many of whom greeted Downing as he returned to Bakewell.

Downing had suffered a gross miscarriage of justice and his conviction was eventually ruled "unsafe" by the Court of Appeal on 15th January 2002. It came to light that Downing had been shaken and his hair pulled during the first round of questioning by police in order to keep him awake. He was not formally cautioned at the time and he was never offered the services of a solicitor. Downing's defence also managed to prove that there was reasonable doubt about the reliability of the confessions made in 1973. The conviction was quashed.

But who did kill Wendy Sewell? Was it one of her lovers? On the day she was attacked, Sewell told her colleagues that she "wanted a breath of fresh air", and went out to take a lunchtime break. She was found by Downing, who raised the alarm and tried to help the injured woman. A policeman arrived on the scene, but instead of calling an ambulance, he let Mrs Sewell struggle to her feet. She stumbled a few feet before falling and hitting her head hard on a gravestone. The attack remains a mystery for Derbyshire police and the victim's friends and family.

# Eve Stratford

(1975)

Eve Stratford was a beautiful 21-year-old bunny girl who appeared as "Girl of the Month" in the March 1975 centrefold of *Mayfair* magazine. It was the naked poses and the quotes she used in the girlie magazine that, the police believe, led to her murder. The interview that accompanied the naked pictures quoted the stunning blonde as saying that she liked to be "dominated sexually but not whipped or tied up". She went on to say that: "I do tend to flirt and tease rather a lot. I just get a kick out of turning men on."

Eve was born in Germany, her mother's homeland, in December 1953, and the family moved around a great deal as her father Albert was in the Medical Corps. They eventually settled in Aldershot, before Stratford moved with her boyfriend Tony Priest, lead singer with the Vineyard, to Leyton in 1972, while her parents retired to Warrington in Lancashire. Three years later, the bunny girl was working at the Playboy Club in Park Lane, London, where she had been recommended for the job by a friend. She was close to her family and was known to talk almost daily with her mother on the phone. Stratford saw herself as one of life's golden girls; she loved wearing gold jewellery and reveled in the high life that came with her job. She had done well at school, passing five "O" Levels, and three "A" levels in German, art and business studies.

The bright lights of London were already beckoning when Stratford and Priest moved to Leyton. Bert Stratford, her older brother, also decided to stay in the southeast. Eve's first jobs in the capital were as a secretary and public relations girl before she found herself a job in a boutique. Stratford then joined the German Tourist Office based in Mayfair, where she stayed for 14 months before her big break to become a bunny girl came along. She joined the Park Lane club as a trainee cocktail bunny on 19th November 1973, and within two weeks was fully trained, earning £1.50 an hour for a 35-hour week with tips of £10 to £15 to top up her salary. In the middle of 1974, Eve was photographed for *Playmate*, in a shoot organized by *Playboy*. She was disappointed when photographer, Brian Hennes, told her that although she could be a potential "Playmate of the Month", she needed to lose some weight. Despite the slight setback, Stratford was determined to make it to the top and was becoming increasingly popular at the Playboy Club, where she was often used in publicity shots. Stratford had a happy demeanour and when asked about her ambitions at the time would say: "to stay as happy as I am now". Her favourite things were seafood, science fiction, Cointreau and Cornwall; the Vineyard, originally called the Onyx, had been formed in the southwest. She and Priest lived with two other members of the Vineyard at their flat in Lyndhurst Drive and it was here that she was found dead by her boyfriend on Tuesday 18th March 1975.

Stratford's throat had been cut and she was found partially clothed, with one ankle bound by a nylon stocking while her hands were tightly bound with a scarf. Although she had been happy to pose for *Mayfair* it was reported that she had not been particularly pleased by the finished article. According to her bunny colleague Christine Howard, who later stated that the dead woman was very unhappy about it, the interview worried the 21-year-old blonde because she thought it made her sound gay. She had admitted to liking both men and women, although she had readily agreed that sexually she preferred men. However, when police began investigating Stratford's untimely death, although they believed the crime was sexually motivated, they weren't sure whether they were looking for a man or a woman. When Eve's feelings about the centrefold were released to the press, Yvonne Fisk, managing director of the *Playboy* rival, was quick to defend the interview, saying that while Stratford may not have stated exactly what was printed, she had signed an agreement saying she was happy with the final edition. Colleagues at the Playboy Club thought the 18 pictures published of Stratford were tastefully done, but many did describe their shock at her outspoken comments about her sex life.

Police were convinced that the magazine piece had probably lured Stratford's killer to her. In it, Stratford stated that she lived alone with her cat Eric, where in fact, she had three housemates. At the time of the murder, Eve was on two months' leave from the club in order to further her modelling career in her desire to become famous. Following Stratford's brutal murder, all members of the band, including their manager Jerry Lordan, were questioned at length by police. All were allowed home.

It was hoped that Stratford's makeshift diary, made up from sheets of notepaper, would trap the killer. Found at the murder scene, the diary listed dozens of names, including many of the men in Eve's life.

In the early days of the investigation, many of them were questioned and cleared of suspicion, but some were difficult for the police to trace. Police were concerned that the murderer was one of Eve's ex-lovers who had been spurned by the would-be model, but they were almost equally convinced that the killer had been turned on by the quotes from Eve in *Mayfair*. They believed that Eve had been spotted in London and followed home to her flat in Lyndhurst Drive before she was brutally murdered. Part of the investigation led police to question other bunny girls from the club, following reports that some of the girls had received obscene phone calls and that one of them, Marilyn Looms, had received death threats following her own nude centrefold in *Mayfair*. Five days after Eve was murdered, it was revealed to the press that she had also had three annoying phone calls on the day she died. Each time she answered the phone the caller said nothing and then cut the line dead. The fourth time the phone rang it was a friend, Debbie Archibald, on the other end of the line. She said that Eve had wondered whether she had had trouble getting through, and told her brother's former girlfriend about the three previous calls. Eve cut the call with Debbie short at around 11.00am, when she told her that she had to dash over to see her agent. Stratford met with her agent, Annie Walker, just hours before she was killed, to arrange a new series of pictures for some promotional literature. Walker reported that Eve was happy and really looking forward to the session. It would prove to be a date with fame that she was never able to keep.

Six months after Stratford was brutally murdered, 16-year-old Lynne Weedon took a short cut that would cost the young girl her life.

Weedon was trying to get to her home in Lampton Avenue, Hounslow, when, on 3rd September 1975, she was beaten over the head with a blunt object, dragged into bushes and raped. The schoolgirl was then thrown over a fence and into the grounds of an electricity substation. The teenager had vowed she would never use the alleyway after dark because it was frequented by prowlers but, after a late night with friends, Weedon did decide to take the shorter route home.

She lay undiscovered for eight hours until the following morning, when she was found by school caretaker Victor Voice who could see, despite her injuries, she was still alive. Weedon died in hospital from her injuries – a fractured skull and a brain haemorrhage – a week later, without having been able to give the police any information about her attacker. More than 400 people offered to help police track down the brutal sex killer. A team of 23 detectives, backed by uniformed officers, interviewed all callers in the hope of finding clues that would catch the killer. However, despite Detective Chief Superintendent Frew's claim that the police were building a profile of the attacker, they were no nearer to finding the murderer.

Just six weeks after Lynne Weedon's murder, detectives were examining new clues in the case of Eve Stratford. An empty bedsit in Liverpool had revealed newspaper reports of the 21-year-old's brutal killing that were smeared with lipstick. Also at the scene were magazine photographs of the young model, which appeared to have been stabbed with a dart. The bizarre evidence was uncovered by a landlord who had been clearing up the flat after it was vacated by two male tenants.

Apart from the fact that both Eve and Lynne were killed in London in the same year, there seemed little to link the two cases. However, as technology in forensic science developed, it was discovered in 2007 that there was DNA on both victims which proved that they had been killed by the same murderer. It was an amazing breakthrough for the authorities and funding was made available to the end of 2011 in order to help the police try and track the killer of two innocent and beautiful young girls.

When pregnant mother-of-two Lynda Farrow was murdered in a frenzied knife attack at the age of 29 in January 1979, the fact that it had been snowing (just as it was when Stratford was murdered) led police to believe that the young mother's death was also connected to that of the murdered bunny girl. That Farrow had, until just prior to her murder, been connected to a gaming club where she had worked as a croupier also gave rise to speculation that the murders were linked. Lynda Farrow was separated from her husband, 32-year-old Paul, with whom she had two young daughters. She was in a new relationship with grocer and market stall trader Fred Gay (37), and the couple were expecting their first baby together. Farrow was 28 weeks' pregnant. On the morning of the attack at her home in Woodford Green, London – not far from where Stratford was murdered – Farrow took her two girls to school before meeting up with her mother. The two women had breakfast together and chatted over a cup of tea before heading out to the shops. Farrow bought some socks for her daughters and a pair of shoes for herself, before kissing her mother goodbye and telling her she would see her soon. Lynda Farrow then went to visit her partner, who was working on his stall, before heading home. She had a lot of household chores to do before she was due to pick up her daughters, Samantha (11) and eight-year-old Justine, from school. The young mother arrived home around 2.30pm and took a phone call in the hallway. She was then brutally attacked by her assailant who cut her throat. When the phone rang again at around 3.00pm, it went unanswered. Farrow's two girls waited for their mother at school, but when she didn't arrive to collect them they headed home alone. After banging on the door they looked through the letterbox and saw their mother lying dead in the hallway.

Although police believed that Farrow's and Stratford's murders were linked and that the murderer could be a gambler, it was thought that the attack on the young mother was not sexually motivated. It was a horrific attack on a young woman who was devoted to her children and her family. No one could believe that she had an enemy who would kill a heavily pregnant young woman. Despite a *Crimewatch* reconstruction of the murder, the case of who murdered Lynda Farrow remains unsolved, alongside the killings of Eve Stratford and Lynne Weedon. However, in January 2009, police were investigating whether Farrow had been murdered by a contract killer due to the way in which the mother was killed; Lynda was stabbed with such ferocity her head was almost severed.

# Renee and Andrew MacRae

(1976)

Born in 1940, Renee MacRae went missing along with her three-year-old son, Andrew, in 1976. This is now Britain's longest running missing persons case and both mother and son are presumed dead. It is believed that Renee and Andrew were murdered, but no one has ever been brought to justice and the case remains open. MacRae and Andrew went missing from their home in Inverness, Scotland. She was separated from her husband, Gordon MacRae (with whom she had an older son, nine-year-old Gordon), who had started divorce proceedings shortly before his wife went missing. Mrs MacRae had been in a five-year relationship with a married man and police set up a confidential telephone line for cheating couples in Inverness who may have had crucial information at the time. But the police were severely hampered by the sea of deceit surrounding the affairs of friends and acquaintances, who were reluctant to come forward with information. MacRae had set off from home in the early evening of 12th November with her two sons. After dropping Gordon with his father, Renee then headed south on the A9 in the direction of Perth. She was due to visit her sister, but the mother and child never arrived at their destination. They have not been seen since.

That same evening, Renee's car was spotted on fire in an isolated lay-by just 10 miles from her home. The train driver who spotted the car raised the alarm, but by the time police arrived, there was no sign of Renee or her small son. A huge police search was implemented, but no trace of the missing woman and her son was found and no clues were left at the scene. Witnesses had seen a man dragging something near the car – it was reported to be a dead sheep – earlier that evening; MacRae had been wearing a sheepskin coat on the day she went missing. Other witnesses told police about a man seen with a pushchair near the quarry. Police suspected foul play and concluded that both had been the victims of murder. It soon became clear, once the investigation got under way, that MacRae had a complicated personal life.

The 36-year-old mother was having a clandestine affair with her husband's married accountant. Gordon MacRae employed father of two, Bill MacDowell, at his Scottish building firm and had no idea of his wife's affair, which was reported to have begun sometime in 1971. It came as somewhat of a blow to find out that MacRae had not been intending to visit her sister that day, but instead was planning to see MacDowell, who happened to be Andrew's biological father. The news was confirmed by Renee's closest friend, Valerie Steventon, who was the only one who knew of the affair between MacDowell and the boss's wife. MacDowell did admit to the affair but denied that he was in any way involved in the case. There was a brief breakthrough in May 1977 when police found what they thought were the pair's corpses in Dalmagarry quarry; however, nothing was proved at the time. In 1980, Gordon MacRae was planning to marry his 29-year-old receptionist Vivian Phillips, but as his wife's body had never been discovered, he was left with the difficult situation of having to divorce a "dead" wife. Two years previously, the investigation had been wound down.

The riddle of missing Renee and Andrew was covered in a Scottish documentary, which brought about a renewed interest in the case and, in 2004, Dalmagarry quarry was excavated. The dig did not provide any new clues or evidence and police are also satisfied that the bodies are not buried under the A9, which was undergoing extensive upgrading at the time of the disappearance. No new evidence has ever come to light and the events surrounding the missing mother and son remain unsolved.

# Bob Crane

(1978)

Forty-nine-year-old entertainer Bob Crane, best known for his role in the hit TV series *Hogan's Heroes*, was found brutally murdered in his apartment on the 29th June 1978 by his friend, the actress Victoria Berry. Having knocked on the door and received no answer, Berry let herself into the unlocked apartment and discovered Crane lying on the bed in his boxer shorts with his head bashed in. His skull was fractured and he had been so badly beaten about the face that he was unrecognizable. Despite a large manhunt for his killer, the case remains unsolved more than 33 years later.

Crane was an aspiring musician during his younger years – he was a talented drummer – but started out in show business as a disc jockey. In June 1978, Crane was on tour in the play *Beginner's Luck*, in Scottsdale, Arizona. After several failed attempts to make a comeback after *Hogan's Heroes* finished in 1971 (including the Disney flop *Superdad*), Crane was hoping to develop a TV sitcom idea at the time of his murder. The day before he was attacked, the entertainer was out bar-hopping with a friend, John Carpenter, who often accompanied Crane to topless bars and strip clubs where both men liked to pick up available women for sex. These sex sessions were often videoed by both men, despite the fact that the actor was married and was also having an affair with the actress Patti Olsen. There was talk at the time that Crane was unhappy about his friendship with Carpenter – a video salesman – and wanted to bring their relationship to an end. However, the two men went out that night as usual.

They picked up two women at the Safari nightclub and separated to have sex with their respective "dates". Sometime later Bob Crane is known to have returned to his apartment alone. When Berry arrived on the scene, someone had clearly entered the room during the night and crushed Crane's skull. A camera tripod was found to be missing and the killer had tied an electric cord around the victim's neck. Police interviewed all Crane's neighbours, but no one had heard anything. There was no forced entry to the apartment and it was quickly surmised that the actor knew his attacker. In addition, a bottle of Scotch was found on the table, although it was never Crane's tipple. As Carpenter had been one of the last people to see Crane alive, he was quickly established as the prime suspect. The video equipment and tapes found in the apartment further convinced police that Carpenter was involved, as both Crane and the video salesman were seen having group sex with different women on the tapes. Further, the car Carpenter was renting was found to have a rare blood type inside, which was a possible match to Crane. There wasn't enough evidence, however, to convict Carpenter of the crime, and this, combined with a badly organized investigation by police, saw Crane's friend walk free.

Nothing further happened until the case was reopened in 1992 when investigators discovered – with the help of developments in DNA – that the tissue deposits found in Carpenter's car matched those of the victim. Carpenter was eventually brought to trial in 1994 but was acquitted. Another theory is that a disgruntled husband, boyfriend or lover of one of Crane's many conquests murdered the actor.

# Genette Tate

(1978)

A massive police hunt began on 19th August 1978 when 13-year-old Genette Tate simply cycled into thin air. The newspaper girl was last seen by two school friends, who confirmed that she stopped to chat for a moment before pedaling around the corner of a country lane in Aylesbeare, near Exeter, Devon, on her afternoon round. Just minutes later, Genette's friends found her bike abandoned in the middle of the road, surrounded by newspapers. More than 100 police officers and 50 villagers took part in the search as fears grew for the young girl's safety. To start with, Detective Chief Superintendent Sharpe, head of Devon and Cornwall CID, was keeping an open mind, although he did admit that the search was on the same scale as a murder hunt. But the case was a complete mystery. There was no sign of an accident or a struggle at the spot where the bike was found.

John Tate, Genette's 36-year-old father, was filled with anguish when the press spoke to him at the family cottage. He was sure that his daughter would not have run away, stating that it just wasn't the sort of thing Genette would do. He also appealed to anyone that might have abducted his daughter to return her safely to her family. Friends Tracey Pratt (14) and 12-year-old Margaret Heavy stated that they had last seen the missing girl moments before they found her abandoned blue-and-white bike on Saturday 19th August. The newspapers Genette had been carrying were scattered everywhere, but the two girls were confident that if the missing girl had been attacked and had screamed out they would have heard her.

Interest in the case was further heightened when Chief Superintendent Reginald Lester, head of Norfolk CID, linked the case, in terms of its similarities, to that of another missing girl, April Fabb, who vanished in April 1969. April, also 13 and also riding a blue-and-white bike, went missing on a country lane in a case that would continue to baffle police. Like Genette, there were only a few minutes between the time the girl was last seen and when her abandoned bike was found. Lester said at the time: "I have never known anything like it. A child has quite literally disappeared – in broad daylight, only yards from her home." He also said that the situation defied belief. April went missing in the tiny hamlet of Metton, Norfolk. Known to be shy and timid, she was on holiday from Cromer Secondary School, and was looking forward to going to Norwich to buy some material for her sewing class. At 10.00am on the day she disappeared, April was dressed in brown trousers and a green jumper. At 12.20pm, she returned from walking the family's Cairn terrier, Trudy. Twenty minutes later, April was given a note from a friend, Susan Dixon, who was unable to make the shopping trip the following day. April was upset and, at her mother's suggestion, headed for the nearby telephone box to phone her friend Gillian Smith to see if she could go instead. At 1.30pm she was back from the telephone box with the answer that her other friend would be able to go into Norwich with her. As she was, by now, much happier, April's mother suggested that she took the cigarettes the young girl was giving her brother-in-law, Bernard, for his birthday over to him in a neighbouring village. Her mother also gave her a blue handkerchief to go with the cigarettes. April went upstairs to change into a red divided skirt. Her hair was up in a brown bow and she was wearing slip-on Scholl sandals. At around 1.40pm, April got on her bike and cycled 200 yards down the road towards her sister's house in Roughton, two and a half miles away. Before she travelled far, the shy girl stopped and spoke to two friends, Christine Dixon and Maureen Hueck, both aged 12. The girls were playing in a field when April stopped, but she was soon on her way to her sister Pam's. At around 2.06pm, she was spotted by farm tractor driver Joseph Livingston-Brown and other witnesses, just by Pill Box crossroads. At 2.15pm, the blue-and-white bike was seen abandoned around 150 yards past the crossroads by three men working on ordnance surveys, but they thought nothing of it and drove on. The bike had been thrown into a field and April had by then been missing for nine minutes (although no one knew this then). The bike was spotted by David Empson and taken to Roughton police station. The cigarettes and handkerchief, along with some small change, were found in the saddlebag. Meanwhile, April's parents had their evening meal, a little put out that their daughter had stayed at her sister's for tea without letting them know. By 7.00pm, however, her mother was beginning to worry. April's father thought that his son-in-law would bring his daughter home at any minute, but at 8.30pm his wife set off on her own bicycle for Pam's house. Fifteen minutes later, Mrs Fabb learned that her youngest daughter never arrived, and the police were involved in an investigation by 10.00pm that evening. The question was asked, where is April Fabb? It's a question that's still being asked today.

On the day she went missing, Genette Tate had been doing a favour for a friend by delivering the evening newspapers. In an emotional appeal, her mother Sheila and stepmother Violet buried their differences and begged whoever was holding Genette to let her go. Four days after she went missing, three of the schoolgirl's friends joined in the hunt and made a dramatic reconstruction of the 13-year-old's last known movements before she disappeared. Both Tracey and Margaret retraced their steps of Saturday 19th August, while another friend, known only as Amanda, cycled Genette's bike for the reconstruction. She admitted to being very nervous but said she desperately wanted to help find her best friend. Ten days after the incident, police issued a photofit of a man they wanted to interview. He was seen driving a maroon car close to the spot where the missing girl vanished, and police, led by Detective Chief Superintendent Eric Rundle, were convinced he had vital information. The car had passed Genette and her friends – in the same direction the schoolgirl took – before she cycled around the bend in the lane. The driver was described as between 18 and 25 years old with thick blackish eyebrows and a pale complexion. He was wearing a light-coloured suit with rolled-up sleeves. But, despite appeals combined with a search by more than 7,000 volunteers, Genette's disappearance remained a mystery.

At the end of August, more than a year later, the police stepped up their hunt for the Pink Panther rapist after it was feared that there were links to Genette. The Pink Panther, so named for a pink scarf he wore over his face during attacks on women, had raped two women at knifepoint near Exeter in August 1979 and had terrorized another woman in her home. An artist's impression of a man who was seen close to where the schoolgirl disappeared was strikingly similar to that of the photofit picture the police had of the rapist. The man, whom police didn't initially identify, had gone missing from his home and it was believed that he'd fled to Grimsby or South Shields. However, it wasn't long before police caught their man – he was named as 39-year-old car dealer James Godfried, who was known to have attacked young girls and women who were out cycling in April 1978. His first victim was a 22-year-old student barrister, whom he attacked the previous year: having knocked her off her bike in Fulham, south London, he then stole her handbag and left her badly injured. That same day, he deliberately drove his car at an 18-year-old au pair in Putney. He then bundled the half-conscious young woman into his car and drove her to a remote spot, before stripping her naked and raping her for which he stood trial at the Old Bailey in August 1979. The au pair was rescued by taxi driver John Mahoney from Hastings, who was later rewarded with £50 by Judge Charles Lawson QC, who praised him for his actions. Although originally from West Ewell in Surrey, Godfried was known to have been only a short distance away from Genette on the day she went missing. Conducting his own defence at the trial, Godfried failed to convince the jury of his innocence, and the 12-strong team, which included eight women, took less than an hour to convict him on seven charges. Sadly for Genette's family, the young girl's disappearance wasn't one of them. Sentenced to 14 years in prison, Godfried blew a kiss to his loyal wife before he was taken to the cells. It wasn't the first time that the rapist had been kept at Her Majesty's pleasure; in 1965 he had been jailed for six years for robbery with violence and indecently assaulting an au pair girl, and it was revealed in newspaper reports that he had been on parole from a sentence for car thefts and forgery when he drove out in search of young girls on bicycles one night in April 1978.

Less than two years following Genette's disappearance her family were still in turmoil. By February 1980, her father and stepmother had separated, as the pain of their loss continued to be too much to bear. The pressures had been building up for the Tate family for more than 18 months and there was still no news on what had happened to Genette. John Tate and his second wife, Violet, had already founded the International Find A Child organization to help families of missing children and it was hoped that the charity wouldn't fold due to the couple's separation. But the family's anguish didn't end with the Tates' subsequent divorce. In May that same year, it was revealed that Genette had been a desperately unhappy child and, after it was discovered that her father had had an illicit sexual relationship with a 10-year-old girl, police began to wonder whether she had simply just run away from home. Although no action was taken at the time, a report was sent to the Director of Public Prosecutions. Genette had shown her distress with life by slashing furniture and starting a fire, and a senior police officer did give an interview to the press in which he stated that it was possible the schoolgirl had run away, although police thinking was that she was most likely to have been abducted. The Tate family then found themselves in the newspapers again in April 1981 in a bizarre courtroom battle where John Tate and Violet Tate both asked for custody of the missing girl should she ever be found. However, Judge Paul Clarke, hearing their applications in Chambers, didn't think it was practical to make an order while Genette was still missing. He continued by confirming a 1975 custody ruling made in favour of John Tate when he divorced from Genette's mother, Sheila.

As with many high-profile cases, and particularly those involving children, there are a number of people who step forward offering help to find missing persons or to help solve the case. Genette's disappearance was no different and, in the early 1980s, a number of mediums made claims about what had happened to the 13-year-old. Frances Dymond from Perranporth in Cornwall, who had helped to find five cadets lost on snowbound Dartmoor in April 1981, came forward to say that she believed Genette had been strangled by a sex maniac before her body was bricked up in his house in the Exeter area. Describing the house as having bay windows and repair work carried out upstairs, the 55-year-old medium went on to state that Genette had hurt her leg as she was dragged from her bike and that the motive for the attack was sexual. Police were keen to stress at the time that Mrs Dymond's information would be evaluated like any other brought to their attention. There were literally hundreds of theories brought forward by mediums and clairvoyants about the case, and potential witnesses who were in the village on the day were questioned under hypnosis, but nothing of any significance came to light. To cause further confusion, although there were those who genuinely wanted to help with this serious crime, there were also those who wanted to "cash-in" on a family's grief. Eleanor McCarron from Teignmouth in Devon was eventually fined £50 for wasting police time and thousands of pounds of public money when she claimed her husband's cousin, David Spiring, had quickly driven away from the village on the day that Genette vanished, hoping that the man she detested would be implicated in the crime.

Five years later, with no real clue as to what had happened to Genette, police received a tip-off from a man in the West Country about a couple who had been in Aylesbeare on the day in question, but had since emigrated to Brisbane in Australia. Although little was known about why this information was of such interest to police, they took it seriously enough for two senior officers to make the long trip down under to hear the couple's story. The couple claimed that a man they knew, who was jailed for life in 1981 for the killing of a 20-year-old hitchhiker near Aylesbeare, had been in the village on the day Genette vanished. Police must have believed that they had a serious chance of closing the case. Meanwhile, John Tate's agony continued when he and his new young wife lost their baby just hours after she had given birth. His torture was further compounded when, in June 1985, an MP demanded that he should be brought to trial for alleged sex offences against the underage girl. The alleged offences had taken place between 1976 and 1978 and Tory MP Geoffrey Dickens, who had been conducting a campaign for several years against child sex abuse – and who had taken up the case after being approached by several senior colleagues from the West Country – called for Tate's prosecution. He also urged the then prime minister, Margaret

Thatcher, to ensure that no government money was directed towards International Find A Child, which was still headed up by Tate. John Tate refused to comment.

In 1986, it was suggested at a unique crisis summit of police chiefs in London, following the horrific murder of schoolgirl Sarah Harper, that one man, or a group of men, were responsible for abducting, abusing, killing and disposing of children. Genette was one of the victims on the list along with Susan Lawrence (14) who went missing from her London home in July 1979 and Martin Allen (15) who disappeared on 5th November that same year. There were 14 top cases on the list, which also included Susan Maxwell (11), murdered in July 1982, and five-year-old Charlotte Hogg, who was found murdered in July 1983. Several factors linked many of the cases together, including the facts that a car was used, there was powerful sexual assault, the body was dumped some miles from the victim's home, and that the perpetrator was quick, clever, ruthless and cool. More than a year later and James Godfried (who had been freed on health grounds) was back in the press, having claimed that he had killed a total of 13 girls and women including Genette Tate. However, police – who interviewed the convicted rapist on the Greek island of Mykonos – were doubtful of his claims. Later, in 1987, Godfried hanged himself in a Greek prison while awaiting trial for the murder of 28-year-old Nancy Connor. The fact that Godfried was on trial for murder in Greece sparked fury in Britain as British doctors had decided that he was "no risk" and he had been freed from prison there seven years early.

The 12-year hunt for missing Genette then took a dramatic turn in October 1990, when a woman claimed she had been in the car with the man who had killed the schoolgirl. She stated that she had watched the man carry the unconscious girl into some woods after his car had knocked her from her bike, and that when he returned he was covered in blood. The man allegedly bragged that he had raped the 13-year-old before burying her body. The man the woman named was an Exeter man in his early 50s who had been drinking heavily at the time of the abduction. The woman was interviewed at length by police and, in a series of tape recordings, claimed: "enough is enough, something has to be done ... keeping this bottled up for 12 years has been like a prison sentence". The woman claimed to have been one of four passengers in a Mini on the day Genette went missing. The occupants decided to take a short cut through winding country lanes after drinking heavily at lunchtime and the woman claimed that Genette was knocked off her bike. All the occupants of the car had been interviewed at the time the case began, but police decided to interview all five again; however, no connections were made to the missing girl.

By the mid-1990s, however, an entirely new man was in the frame. Robert Black became notorious as Britain's worst serial child-killer, who boasted about the 40 young girls he cruelly abused in the years before he turned to murder. He was questioned by police about Genette and gave details to the Channel 4 *Dispatches* programme about how the 13-year-old was grabbed from her bike and bundled into a vehicle. The former van driver gave chilling accounts of the young girls he had killed and said: "Somebody once said to me that their motto was

'When they're big enough, they are old enough.' I tended to agree with that. I love children but I don't want to hurt them. Therefore, if I don't want to hurt them they'd have to be dead." Black turned out to be the killer of Susan Maxwell, Caroline Hogg and 10-year-old Sarah Harper. Having been convicted, Black was sentenced to 10 life sentences and directed to serve a minimum of 35 years. Forty-seven-year-old Black showed no emotion in court and only spoke when he sneered, "Well done boys" to police officers as he was led away. Although Black's conviction brought what little comfort it could to the grieving families of Susan, Caroline and Sarah, he refused to see John Tate, who desperately wanted to know if Genette had also been a victim. It was 18 years since the abduction and Tate could find no rest, even though Black was suspected of other unsolved crimes. Black sent a terse note to Tate, which stated, "I have nothing to say." He later denied any involvement in Genette's disappearance, although DNA taken from one of her jumpers 24 years after her abduction turned out to be inconclusive when tested against Robert Black, who was proved to have been in east Devon at the time of the attack. Black was again quizzed by police years later as they had long suspected that he was involved.

In 2003, 25 years after Genette disappeared, her family and the police were convinced that she was dead, yet the case remained open and hope still held out that her killer would be found. In April 2005, Black was arrested while in prison on suspicion of murdering Genette and was taken for questioning at a top-security police station in Leeds. He had twice before been interviewed in prison and refused to answer questions, so a move was made and Home Office permission granted for him to be removed from jail for questioning. But there was insufficient evidence linking Black to murder and, in 2008, the case against the Scottish van driver dealt a devastating blow to the Tate family and the police when prosecutors decided they could not charge him with the crime. In 2011, Black was still the prime suspect for the killing of Genette and April Fabb and was suspected of killing at least 12 more children in the UK and France before his capture in 1990.

The biggest ever missing persons inquiry that Britain had ever seen, a £1,000 reward offered in 1978 for information, and 7,000 members of the public desperately trying to help trace the missing schoolgirl all failed to turn up any clues that would lead to what had happened to the elfin-faced teenager. The case remains open and while it has long been suspected that Genette Tate is sadly no longer alive, the hope that her killer will one day be identified lives on.

# Carl Bridgewater

(1978)

Carl Bridgewater's parents still visit the grave of their son every two weeks as well as on special days such as birthdays and anniversaries. It's been more than 33 years since their 13-year-old son was shot dead while carrying out his paper round, but the schoolboy they nicknamed "Atom" due to the enormous amount of energy he had is not forgotten. Janet and Brian Bridgewater are still grieving for the vivacious little boy, who was kind and willing to help anyone. They are still struggling to cope with what happened to their cherished son, although they have given up hope that the killer will be brought to justice.

It was 19th September 1978 and Carl had just been to the dentist with his mother, brother and sister. He had left the dentist's ahead of his family as he needed to get back and start his paper round in Prestwood, Staffordshire. At one of the last stops on his paper round – Yew Tree Farm – approximately three miles northwest of Stourbridge in the Midlands – Carl was surprised to find a door at the farmhouse open as he approached with their newspaper. As elderly cousins Mary Poole and Fred Jones were disabled, Carl was used to opening a door to the farmhouse, letting himself in and leaving their newspaper on a chair. Knowing he would be welcome, Carl made his way into the house. What he didn't know was that the couple were not at home and that the farm was, in fact, in the middle of being burgled. Upon entering the house, Carl was forced into the living room, where he was shot in the head at point-blank range. His lifeless body was found by a friend of the elderly owners who had just dropped by at 5.30pm. It was less than an hour since the paperboy had died. The police investigation, headed up by Detective Chief Superintendent Bob Stewart, was horrified by the merciless killing of a young boy. More than 50 police officers were quickly assigned to comb the nearby area, and comments from police at the time suggested that Carl might have been silenced because he recognized someone present at the farm that day.

When Carl didn't appear for his dinner, his parents were worried and his father went out to look for him. Brian Bridgewater went past Yew Tree Farm and discovered many policemen on the scene. He had no idea what had happened and didn't realize that his son lay dead in the house. It wasn't until the police knocked on the couple's door that they discovered the horrendous truth of why their son hadn't made it home in time for the family's evening meal.

At the same time that the family were facing total shock, they also had to cope with the media circus that quickly descended on their usually quiet home life. Police were placed outside the house to keep journalists and other interested parties back, while they were advised to keep their curtains closed and to turn up the television so that people outside couldn't hear what was being said. The Bridgewaters had little choice but to try and cope; both for the sake of their other children and the fact that the fairly crime-free area in which they lived was now besieged by photographers and camera crews.

Four men were eventually arrested for the murder of Carl Bridgewater. Nicknamed the Bridgewater Four, the men were tried and found guilty of killing the teenage paperboy. Patrick Molloy was first arrested in November 1978 following a similar robbery at a farmhouse in Romsley, just 10 miles away from where Carl was murdered. However, Molloy denied killing the schoolboy and although he admitted to being present at the house, he claimed he was robbing an upstairs room at the time Carl was shot. He stated that he heard a gunshot downstairs. Not long after Molloy's arrest, three other men – Jim Robinson, and Michael and Vincent Hickey (who were cousins) – were also arrested in connection with the murder and robbery. The Bridgewater Four insisted on their innocence but while Molloy was found guilty of manslaughter and sentenced to 12 years' imprisonment, the three others were convicted of murder. Robinson and Vincent Hickey were both sentenced to life imprisonment and recommended to serve a minimum of 25 years each. Michael Hickey was only 17 at the time of the murder and, while he was still detained in prison, it was suspected that his sentence would be shorter than that of Robinson and his 25-year-old cousin Vincent, who had admitted to being at the farmhouse on the day that Carl was shot.

In 1981, at the age of 51, Molloy died in prison of a heart attack, but Robinson and the two Hickey men fought a campaign for release on the grounds of their innocence, which was led by Michael Hickey's mother, Ann Whelan, and journalist Paul Foot, a high-profile campaign writer. Foot played a prominent role in campaigns to overturn other convictions, including that of the Birmingham Six, and took an active interest in the convictions of Abdelbaset al-Megrahi for the Lockerbie bombing and James Hanratty for the A6 murder, for whom he tried unsuccessfully to gain a posthumous pardon. An earlier appeal by the Bridgewater Four in 1989 had proved unsuccessful. Foot was successful in his campaign to get the Birmingham Six released in 1991 and was instrumental in gaining freedom for the Hickey cousins and Robinson in 1997 when their convictions were also overturned by the Court of Appeal on the grounds that the trial had been unfair in their second appeal hearing. This ruling came about when the Court of Appeal decided that certain evidence had been fabricated by police in order to help persuade Molloy to make an initial confession. However, it was noted by the Court of Appeal judges that Vincent Hickey's admission that he was at the farm that day made a retrial – which could reveal evidence on which a jury could convict if properly directed – possible. The Crown Prosecution Service decided against this, however, leaving Carl Bridgewater's family with little hope of justice. The appeals by the Bridgewater Four had left the victim's family devastated.

At the time that Patrick Molloy was questioned by police following the murder, another suspect, Hubert Spencer, was also brought in for questioning. Thirty-eight-year-old Spencer – an ambulance driver – lived in Wordsley, close to the Bridgewater family, and drove a blue Vauxhall Viva. A blue car matching the description of Spencer's car was seen at the farm on the day of the murder, while witnesses described the driver as being in uniform. Spencer was eliminated from police inquiries when Molloy and his accomplices were arrested. However, he was convicted of murdering Hubert Wilkes, a 70-year-old farmer on a neighbouring farm not long after Carl's murder took place, and was jailed for life in 1980. He was paroled in 1995.

Carl Bridgewater had only been doing the paper round for two months when his young life was cut tragically short. While his memory will live on deep in the heart of his family, the hope that justice will be done is a long time dead.

# Suzy Lamplugh

(1986)

A simple note in a diary which read: "12.45. Mr Kipper. 37 Shorrolds Road. O/S", was the only clue that police had to go on when 25-year-old Suzy Lamplugh went missing on 28th July 1986. It was feared that the beautiful, blue-eyed estate agent had been lured to 37 Shorrolds Road, which was up for sale at the asking price of £130,000, under false pretenses by a bogus house buyer. Detective Superintendent Nick Carter stated to the press two days later that: "She has been missing for two nights and it's her mother's 50th birthday today. She would never miss that unless something has happened to her."

Police thought that Mr Kipper rang the young woman at the estate agency where she worked, in Fulham Road, west London, on Monday 28th July in the morning, telling her he wished to view the house in Shorrolds Road. Just before 12.45pm, Lamplugh told her boss, Mark Curdon, she was off to an appointment – that was the last her colleagues saw of her. Suzy hadn't taken full particulars of the potential client, and he hadn't been in to register, but as colleague Stephanie Flower (22) explained at the time, this wasn't unusual, as often people would phone the estate agency after having seen a sign outside a house for sale. There had never been any incidents before and there was no reason to suspect that this potential sale was any different to previous ones.

With nothing much to go on, except the note in her diary – and as Suzy was known to have been dyslexic, it's possible that the name she wrote was spelt incorrectly – police launched an investigation into what had happened to the young woman. There was some speculation that Suzy had a new man in her life at the time she went missing – his name was later cited as John Cannan. Statements from Suzy's family and friends and some former contacts of Cannan's clearly pointed at the time to the pair having had a relationship. Cannan was known to have frequented the bars of Fulham, where he liked to chat up women. It's possible that this is how Suzy met Cannan (if they did meet); she had certainly told friends and her mother of her new man, who was "exciting but scary". In fact, Cannan was on day release from Wormwood Scrubs prison where he was in the fifth year of an eight-year sentence for rape. Although attractive and charming, Cannan was renowned for his violent outbursts and sexual perversions. If he was the man that Suzy was now seeing, she had already decided that he was too dangerous, and had told her mother on the morning of the day she disappeared that she was going to dump him. Suzy had mentioned to friends that her new man had connections with Bristol; Cannan was later convicted of killing Shirley Banks in that city in October 1987. However, at the time Suzy went to meet with Mr Kipper, the connection was unknown, although witnesses did report seeing her arguing with a man in Shorrolds Road on 28th July.

But, by 1st August 1986, police were linking Suzy's disappearance to a frenzied sex attacker who had already sexually assaulted three women within 18 months in the Richmond area of London. The likeness of the photofit of the man seen with Suzy and that of the sex attacker were strikingly similar. Victims of the Richmond attacker had had a razor blade held to their throats. After the argument in Shorrolds Road, Suzy Lamplugh was seen getting into her white Ford Fiesta; it was found that night close to another house on the estate agent's books. It was presumed that she took Mr Kipper to see this house too. Meanwhile, police failed to find a policewoman who looked enough like the missing woman to carry out a reconstruction, and no more evidence was forthcoming in the link between the bogus house buyer and the Richmond attacker.

As in other high-profile cases, mediums and psychics came forward to help with the investigation, including the famous Doris Stokes. Diana and Paul Lamplugh were still convinced at this stage that they would see their beautiful daughter again, stating in the *Daily Mirror* that: "We still have faith in the search for our daughter." Mr Lamplugh, a solicitor with the Law Society, went on to say that there had been 1,500 calls from the public offering to help in the search for Suzy. When the estate agent went missing, her younger sister, Tami Lamplugh, was working in New Zealand where she had received a number of letters from Suzy. It was thought at the time that these letters might hold vital clues as to what had happened on the fateful day because the letters – which were sent about once a week – mentioned a number of names. The letters were sent home in Tami's luggage, which then went missing at Heathrow airport. While police began questioning more than 1,600 people, Detective Superintendent Nick Carter was beginning to feel that things were not looking good and was increasingly fearful that the 25-year-old would be found dead.

Just one month after Suzy went missing it was feared that Mr Kipper had struck again when secretary Sarah Lambert vanished in August 1986 after accepting a new job offer from a bogus employer. Lambert had attended a job interview with a man calling himself Mr J Simmons, who claimed he was a property developer. Accepting the £12,000-a-year job, Sarah Lambert turned up at Ealing station the next day, as agreed with Simmons, and phoned her parents to say that she would be going away to the Crown Hotel in Amersham, Buckinghamshire, for a working weekend. The 25-year-old didn't arrive at the hotel, and the description of the man seen with Sarah was similar to that of Kipper – dark hair, tanned and smartly dressed.

The hunt for Suzy Lamplugh continued and, by the end of August 1986, police believed that she had been lured into having a champagne lunch by Kipper before she was kidnapped. Witnesses saw a man of Kipper's description standing outside the house she had agreed to show him with a bottle of champagne sporting a red, white and blue ribbon. A new witness told police that Suzy had looked relaxed and happy and gave a new description to police, which provided a new photofit of the suspect. On the day she went missing there were three sightings of Suzy. The first witness saw her standing outside the house in Shorrolds Road at 12.50pm holding keys. She was alone. Just minutes later, a second witness saw Suzy and Kipper – described as a public-school type – outside the house. The third sighting of Suzy came from a friend of the estate agent, who saw her driving along Fulham Palace Road towards Hammersmith in her office car. There was a man sitting in the passenger seat, but the witness was sure that Suzy didn't look distressed, although she did look serious. Police believed that Suzy's car – which was found at 10.00pm that night in nearby Stevenage Road – had been abandoned between 3.00pm and 5.00pm earlier that day. Three weeks after she went missing, the police investigation hadn't thrown up anything of significance that would help to find the missing woman. There were many theories that were being thought through by police. But the facts show that Suzy probably didn't show Kipper around the house in Shorrolds Road. Eyewitness accounts mean that it would have been the speediest house showing in history. There just wasn't time. It is thought that Suzy received the phone call from Kipper making the appointment on the morning she went missing but there is actually no evidence to back this – it's possible the appointment was made earlier. One theory was that Suzy drove her car to the house, but none of the witnesses remember seeing her car there. The fact that Suzy was spotted looking happy and relaxed with a man holding a bottle of champagne, that she was seen nearly two hours later, and that she had not contacted her office at all during this time gave the police more questions than answers.

Meanwhile, the hunt for Sarah Lambert came to an end on 21st August 1986 when she returned home, unharmed. Lambert had been staying in two Surrey hotels with a man calling himself Simmons, and was apparently unaware that a nationwide hunt had taken place for her when fears were sparked that she had become the second victim of Kipper.

On Friday 21st August, it was becoming clear that there were links between Suzy and a man that the *Daily Mirror* claimed it could identify.

The man, who bore a striking resemblance to Kipper, was educated at a private school and was known to have dated Suzy at least twice after meeting her in a wine bar. The man had also lived in Shorrolds Road; he quit his job on the day Suzy disappeared, changed his address, and told different friends he would be holidaying at different locations. His name was included among the 200 found in Suzy's diary, which police checked thoroughly.

Diana Lamplugh became a desperately worried mother on a mission. For Diana and Paul, the first few months in which Suzy was missing were testing and trying, but they were not unproductive. The couple launched the Suzy Lamplugh Trust on 4th December 1986 in order to raise money to improve the personal safety of women in Britain. When Diana was interviewed about the trust, she confirmed to the press that Suzy's flat had been sold, although the money from the sale was being held by the court until the case was solved. She went on to state that, having been to Suzy's flat, it was obvious that she hadn't intended to "run away". Her personal possessions including her clothes, books and other items were returned to the family's home in East Sheen. The family still hadn't given up hope that Suzy would be found safe and well, although the discovery of a torso – which turned out not to be the remains of their daughter – had caused them considerable stress when it was found earlier in the year. Talking about the Lamplugh Trust, Diana stated: "We want to improve the personal security of working women through research and advice." The trust was some comfort for the family at a time when it was hard to find any, and Diana described herself as: "The living evidence of other people's support." At the time the trust was launched, the plan was to raise £450,000, with the objective to carry out research to enable women of all ages – particularly employees – to fulfill their potential safely.

In January 1987 detectives flew to Belgium to question a new suspect in the case called Mr Kiper (pronounced Keeper), following the discovery of a BMW car – seen close to the area where Suzy went missing – abandoned in St John's Wood in November 1986. The owner of the car, a wealthy globetrotting diamond merchant, was away on business when his address was traced to Antwerp, and family members vowed to clear his name. The lead had come to light when a man living in St John's Wood, Richard Ward, traced Mr Kiper after wanting to buy the car and, realizing the significance of the name, informed police. When the police did eventually catch up with Mr Kiper (also known as David Rosengarten) they were less than satisfied with his story. However, he was cleared after eight hours of questioning in Antwerp by Scotland Yard detectives. Both David Rosengarten and his aunt claimed that the car had been stolen from the Belgian resort of Knokke-Heist.

Then, in November 1987, police had what they thought was a breakthrough when they linked the disappearance of Suzy to that of a vanished bride, Shirley Banks, in Bristol. The suspects in both cases had similar descriptions, and black BMW cars figured in both investigations. Police believed there was a serious connection between the two crimes. Shirley Banks went missing in October 1987 in Bristol while late night shopping. It then struck all concerned that Suzy had once had a mystery boyfriend with Bristol connections, and car salesman and convicted rapist John Cannan (33) was remanded in custody by magistrates, accused of stealing Shirley's Mini. He was also charged with assault with intent to rob a shop assistant in Leamington Spa. In 1994, Suzy Lamplugh was officially declared dead, although the case remains open and her body has never been found. Diana Lamplugh, through her work with the Lamplugh Trust, kept her daughter's case in the public eye, and the family and Trust believed by 1998 that Suzy's killer was in prison for the murder of another woman. The prime suspect and convicted killer was John Cannan.

In May 2000, the Suzy Lamplugh case was reopened. At the time, police believed that they had evidence that would lead them to the secret grave of the missing woman on a disused Army barracks in the Midlands. Using state-of-the-art radar equipment in a bid to pinpoint where she was buried, officers carried out a search at the centre of the site. The device used bounced electrical pulses into the ground, where a signal was then displayed, revealing cavities and disturbed soil. The police were hoping that any dramatic developments in one of Britain's most baffling criminal mysteries would lead to Cannan being interviewed again in connection with Suzy's death and bring justice for her family. However, all efforts failed to shed any light and no body was found. Undeterred, the police then tested DNA samples found in Suzy's car against those of rapists and murderers later that same month, when a new witness came forward claiming to have seen the estate agent being driven in her car by a stranger at the time she was abducted. Detectives believed that microscopic particles of skin and hair discovered in the white Ford Fiesta could trap the murderer. Although he denied any involvement in the case, Cannan was on the list and still remained the prime suspect as far as police were concerned. Once the case was reopened, police also suspected that the perpetrator had an accomplice. By December 2000, John Cannan was interviewed for a fourth time when, not for the first time, it was discussed how much of a resemblance the convicted killer bore to the photofit of Kipper. He had only been out on day release from Wormwood three times when Suzy disappeared 14 years earlier. Police were given special permission by the Home Office to hold Cannan, who was brought to London from his prison cell in York and interviewed under caution. The police also looked at other unsolved murders in their quest to find answers. This fresh probe yielded important clues, including witnesses, and forensic evidence that had simply not been possible in the late 1980s. But the investigation remained long and complex. The case took another turn at the end of 2000 when detectives launched a massive new search for Suzy's body at an old brickworks next to the M5 at Norton, near Worcester, following a tip-off. The brickworks was just several hundred yards from the former Army barracks that the police had already searched, but fresh evidence was enough to convince detectives that they had been looking in the wrong place. Four months later, the police began a new search in the Quantock Hills area of Somerset at a spot known as Dead Woman's Ditch, where the body of newly wed Shirley Banks had been found 13 years earlier. According to newspaper reports at the time, police believed that they had good reason to shift the focus of their search and, in November 2002, headlines read: "We know this man killed

Suzy ... help us to nail him." The picture that accompanied the news showed John Cannan, and police claimed to be closer than ever to charging the convicted murderer. Unfortunately, key evidence was missing from the case, although police strongly believed that people – yet to come forward – knew things that could help them find justice for Suzy's family. Just six months earlier, a dossier was filed with the Crown Prosecution Service recommending that Cannan be charged, but lawyers decided after five months of deliberations that there was still not enough evidence against him. Cannan refused to give the police any clues, despite the fact that his ex-girlfriend, Gilly Paige, claims that he confessed to her that he raped and killed Suzy.

The case was back in the press in 2006 when a breakthrough in DNA technology threatened to expose Cannan as Suzy's killer. Forensic experts took a tiny speck of DNA found in her car from which they grew a larger piece which could be examined in more detail. It was hoped that it would lead to the conviction of the imprisoned Cannan for her murder. The small speck was unusable for testing, however, as the mere act of analysing it would have destroyed it. Then, later that year, it was discovered that Steve Wright, the Ipswich Ripper (also known as the Suffolk strangler and responsible for the deaths of five women) had worked with Suzy Lamplugh on a cruise liner in the 1980s where she was a beautician. Wright was a steward on the *Queen Elizabeth II* and it was believed that the two were friends before Suzy quit a life at sea to return to London in 1985. It turned out that Wright was on shore leave when Suzy disappeared, but he was ruled out of the police investigation into the case in May 2008. The investigation led police back to Worcester in 2010, when they began a new search for Suzy's body in a remote field just to the east of where they originally began digging – at the Norton Army barracks in December 2000. No new clues were discovered at the excavation.

Diana Lamplugh died at the age of 75 on 18th August 2011 without really finding out what happened to her daughter. While the trust she set up may not have given the brave mother of Suzy all the comfort she needed following her daughter's disappearance some 25 years earlier, Diana Lamplugh knew that she had founded one of the most important and influential organizations and had worked tirelessly for more than a quarter of a century in the fight to safeguard people. The Lamplughs were both awarded an OBE for their hard work and their commitment to the trust.

# Linda Cook

(Cinderella Murder, 1986)

Just after midnight on 9th December 1986, Linda Cook left a friend's house in Sultan Road, in the Buckland area of Portsmouth, to walk about a mile home to Victoria Road North. The 24-year-old barmaid was living with Linda Gray, the mother of her boyfriend of five months, while he was on remand in a detention centre. There had been a number of sexual assaults carried out in the crime-ridden area over the preceding few months, but few would have believed the ferocity of the attack on the young woman that night. Linda was walking adjacent to Lake Road, heading south towards the Southsea area of the city, when she was viciously raped and strangled on Merry Row, a piece of wasteland, close to Church Road. She was less than halfway home.

The "Cinderella" murder, as the case became known, saw a bungled attempt by police, under huge pressure to bring about a quick arrest due to the heinous nature of the crime, that was to lead to one of the most notorious miscarriages of justice within the British legal system. What was known about the young woman's movements was that, according to Gray, Linda Cook had left her home sometime before 11.30pm to visit her friend. Her body was discovered the following day and it was quickly established that she had been attacked somewhere between 12.30am and 1.00am in an onslaught that would have lasted around 15 minutes. When Linda was found, she was naked and not wearing her underwear; this was found nearby and taken away for testing. Her nails were long and unbroken, showing no real signs of any kind of struggle on her part. However, the damage suffered by the victim was particularly brutal. Not only had Linda Cook been raped and strangled, but her attacker had stamped on her many times and so severely that her spine and jaw were fractured. Her larynx was crushed and the imprint of a training shoe was found on her stomach. The shoe print was the first real clue that the police were able to gather and it was crucial that the imprint was quickly matched with the shoe and its owner. The case was soon dubbed the "Cinderella" murder when police revealed the evidence they had against the attacker, and the fact that they were looking for a matching pair of trainers.

Meanwhile, forensic tests carried out on the victim showed that there were traces of semen in the vagina and anus. The traces on the victim gave police a vital lead in form of the killer's blood type, and a manhunt for the murderer of Linda Cook was quickly under way.

That same night, 18-year-old able seaman Michael Shirley went to Joanna's nightclub in Southsea, where he met a local girl by the name of Deena Fogg (although she told him her name was Sue). The couple spent the latter part of the evening together before deciding to head to Fogg's home. They took a taxi from outside the club at around 12.25am, and by 12.30am were outside a tower block where Fogg left the vehicle to go and retrieve her child from her mother's flat. It turned out that Fogg had no intention of taking Shirley home with her and, having collected her child, made her way out of the building by another exit, where she gave him the slip and made her own way home. Shirley had the choice to return to his ship, *HMS Apollo*, once he realized that

Fogg wasn't returning to the taxi, but after 15 minutes of waiting he paid the fare and decided to try and find the mother on foot. Shirley spent around 10 minutes trying to find Fogg before heading back to his ship, where he signed in at 1.45am, having taken another taxi from Edinburgh Road at around 1.23am. He saw Fogg a couple of days later and they had a brief conversation, but made no plans to see each other again. Shirley then travelled to Leamington Spa where he spent Christmas with his parents before going back to Portsmouth in January 1986. *HMS Apollo* was bound for the Falkland Islands where she had been patrolling the South Atlantic in the aftermath of the Falklands War, but just before she sailed Michael Shirley went back to Joanna's nightclub on 5th January. Unbeknown to the able seaman, Fogg had been earmarked by police as a potential witness during house-to-house enquiries during the murder investigation. When he returned to Joanna's, Deena Fogg identified Shirley as the man she had been with on the night of the murder and he was arrested by police. Taken into custody, Shirley was then charged with Linda's murder and placed on remand at Winchester prison.

Despite the fact that Linda Cook had no breaks, tears or chips to her nails, the fact that Shirley had numerous scratches over his body weighed heavily as evidence as far as the police were concerned. Shirley also owned a pair of trainers – of the right size – with the distinctive tread as worn by the murderer. He also had the same blood type as the killer. The police, it seemed, had their man. The trial began on 18th January 1987 with Shirley pleading his innocence. With purely circumstantial evidence and no forensic evidence to back up the prosecution's claims of Shirley's guilt, the defence legal team were quite sure that the 18-year-old sailor would be found not guilty. However, the prosecution valiantly satisfied the jury of Shirley's guilt, the judge strongly hinted that he wanted a quick verdict, and within six and a half hours Shirley was convicted and sentenced to life imprisonment. It was a shock to Shirley, his family and his legal team. An appeal was launched, but was rejected by the judge, Sir David Croom-Johnson, in May 1989.

However, there were those – including journalist Neil Humber – who strongly believed that Shirley wasn't guilty of this heinous crime. On two occasions Shirley spent weeks on hunger strike in order to attract attention to his case, and he even staged a rooftop protest. Eventually, prison authorities allowed Shirley and Humber to meet and it was discovered, through the journalist's campaign for the convicted man's release, that Deena Fogg had given two wildly contrasting statements to the police. There were huge discrepancies in the timings that she had given in both statements. In January 1993, Shirley started a 42-day hunger strike in order to make himself "heard", and eventually the Home Office agreed to think about reviewing the case if new evidence was brought to light. By this time, DNA testing was one surefire way to show Shirley's innocence, and he made a plea for this new form of technology to help in his case. Meanwhile, Hampshire police were keen not to reveal how badly they had bungled the case in their efforts to find the killer. Evidence was either "missing" or "had been destroyed" and there seemed nothing much that anyone could do to help Shirley. However, Humber was determined, and agreed to write

# Daily Mirror

See To-day's 'DAILY MAIL.'

THE MORNING JOURNAL WITH THE SECOND LARGEST NET SALE.

No. 1,286. Registered at the G. P. O. as a Newspaper. FRIDAY, DECEMBER 13, 1907. One Halfpenny.

## CAMDEN TOWN MURDER MYSTERY: ROBERT WOOD ON TRIAL FOR HIS LIFE AT THE NEW BAILEY.

The curtain rose on the third act in the Camden Town murder drama yesterday when Robert Wood, an artist, was put in the dock at the Central Criminal Court and tried for the murder of Emily Dimmock on the night of September 11. (1) Robert Wood, the accused man. (2) Emily Dimmock, the murdered woman. (3) Ruby Young, the accused man's sweetheart, who is the principal witness for the prosecution. (4) Mr. Marshall Hall, the leading counsel for the defence. (5) Mr. Arthur Newton, the pri-

soner's solicitor, who prepared the defence, and who defended Wood during the magisterial hearing. (6) The crowd outside the New Bailey watching the entrance of Ruby Young, who is under one of the umbrellas seen in the photograph. (7) Mr. Justice Grantham, the presiding Judge. (8) Sir Charles Mathews, who is prosecuting on behalf of the Crown.—(Elliott and Fry, Grenowell, Bassano, and London Stereoscopic.)

**Marion Gilchrist (1908)** Marion Gilchrist, brutally murdered during a robbery in Glasgow. Oscar Slater was convicted of the crime but later released and acquitted after his cause was championed by renowned author Sir Arthur Conan Doyle.

Oscar Slater pictured during his trial at the High Court in Edinburgh.

**Caroline Luard (Seal Chart Murder, 1908)** Caroline Luard, pictured driving with her husband, was the victim of a seemingly senseless and vicious murder in August 1908.

PHOTOGRAPH OF MRS. C. E. LUARD, THE VICTIM OF THE SEVENOAKS SUMMER HOUSE TRAGEDY.

The inquest on the body of Mrs. Luard, the victim of the Sevenoaks summer-house crime, was opened yesterday afternoon. In the above photograph, taken a few months ago, Mrs. Luard (marked with a cross) is seen in a motor-car driving with her hu— . Major-General C. E. Luard.—("Daily Mirror" photograph.)

**Joseph Wilson (1911)** Police search the area near Lintz Green station for clues (top), following the murder of stationmaster Joseph Wilson (inset) in October 1911, while the coroner examines the scene of the tragedy (bottom).

POLICE AT WORK ON THE MYSTERIOUS MURDER NEAR DURHAM.

Mystery surrounds the murder of Mr. George Wilson, the station-master at Lintz Green, Durham. He was shot dead after sand had been thrown in his eyes as he was entering his house, near the station. No one saw the crime committed, and a booking clerk, who ran to Mr. Wilson's assistance on hearing a gun-shot, was the only witness at the inquest. (1) Police beating a wood in search of a weapon or some other clue. (2) The coroner examining the scene of the tragedy. The portrait is of Mr. Wilson. *(Daily Mirror photograph.)*

# "GREEN BICYCLE" MURDER CHARGE.

Miss Annie Bella Wright.

The scene of the discovery. Inset P.C. Hall.

An arrest has been made in connection with the death, last July, of Annie Bella Wright, in a lonely road at Leicester. Police-Constable Hall discovered that a bullet...

**Bella Wright (Green Bicycle Case, 1919)** Bella Wright (left) was found dead in a quiet country lane in Leicestershire (right) in March 1920, but it was the persistence of PC Alfred Hall (inset) which led to the realization that a murderer was on the loose.

Ronald Light (right), the young mathematical master, who is charged with the murder of Annie Bella Wright, listening intently to the opening statement made by Mr. Sims on behalf of the Crown.

The accused, Ronald Light (right), listens to the prosecution's opening statement.

# TWO YEARS AGO, DON HALE'S
# HIM A HERO. NOW A TV DRA
# AND CASTS DOUBT ON THE MA

By BARBARA
DAVIES

ON THE 30th anniversary of
her murder, television crews
filming at the municipal
cemetery where Wendy Sewell
was battered to death tactfully
chose to withdraw.

When they returned, a small wooden
cross had been crudely stuck into the
ground at the spot where she fell.
Alongside it were some flowers and a
note: "Wendy Sewell, not forgotten".

The fruits of their labours will be
screened across Britain at 9pm
tomorrow in the BBC drama In Denial
Of Murder.

The two-part film returns to the unsolved, mysterious murder of
32-year-old Wendy, the so-called
Bakewell Tart, who died on September
14, 1973, two days after she was attacked.

But in resurrecting the events which
surrounded her death, the BBC is not
so much opening up old wounds as
reminding us that in the close-knit
Derbyshire community of Bakewell
they never healed in the first place.

There has been no closure for Stephen
Downing, who served 27 years for
Wendy's murder before his conviction
was quashed two years ago.

And Don Hale, the Matlock Mercury
editor who campaigned for nearly a
decade to free him, has had little cause
to celebrate, either.

When Downing walked out of jail in
January 2001, it looked as if justice had
finally been served. Hale was feted and
his dogged efforts rewarded with an
OBE and journalistic awards.

But a reinvestigation by police last
year raised further questions about
Downing's innocence and landed Hale
as misguided, if well-intentioned.

The BBC's new drama is yet another
setback for the two men whose
lives became irrevocably entangled as they fought the British
justice system.

Hale is horrified at aspects of
the final version, which portrays
him as a naive, blundering fool
who helped free a man who may
not – after all – be innocent.

"It fails to provide a wholly
accurate version of events," he
says. "Several crucial elements of
the story have been omitted.

"It's not a factual documentary.
This is drama written for
prime-time TV.

"Stephen Tumpkinson has me
saying and doing several things
that never really happened. I
have no complaint against him because
he is tied to the script, but I have never
referred to Wendy Sewell as the
Bakewell Tart."

For Downing, the drama comes on
the back of a series of allegations and
police statements which have left a
cloud of suspicion hanging over him.

The air of triumph which
surrounded his release evaporated a year ago when
Derbyshire Police insisted
he was still the only one of
22 possible suspects they
could not rule out.

"If the law had been
changed and it was possible
to retry Mr Downing, we
would be putting that
evidence to the CPS," they
said, in a statement which
suggested they believed they
had had the right man all along.

Then law firm receptionist Josie
Fisher told police she had been
subjected to obscene phone calls and
letters from Downing when he was in
prison in 1996. Downing denied the calls
were obscene but his phone cards were

BATTERED: Wendy

confiscated. Most damaging of all,
however, was Downing's relationship
with clairvoyant Christine Smith after
his release.

She later produced taped phone
conversations in which she claimed
Downing, 47, confessed to Wendy's
murder. The tapes were
handed to police and
dismissed as "insignificant"
but they made headline news.

It makes my life very
difficult," says Downing. "I
have difficulty finding work
and it's hard knowing that
some people still think I did
it. I have learnt to live with
it. I'm not sure how the
BBC are going to portray
me, so I'm a bit nervous. It
would have been nice to
have been consulted."

He is still living in Bakewell, but he
has moved out of the home he once
shared with his father Ray, his mother
Juanita and sister Christine, into a flat.

"Just about everybody in Bakewell
has welcomed me back," he says.

"People have been very supportive. I
don't get stopped in the street so much
now, but there's still people that
recognise me."

He has been denied the "normal" life
he once dreamt of.

"Things that have been said about me
mean my life very difficult," he says.

"It's hard to find work. My ambition
was to be a cameraman or a freelance
photographer in the media. It's something that I enjoy. I was offered a job
at the Nottingham Evening Post, but
I decided that it would be a bit too
much for me."

The intense closeness he once shared
with Hale has gone.

"Don and I are in touch, but only by
phone at the moment," he says. "We
still consider ourselves to be friends.
We've become a bit more distant.
It's not the same relationship we had
when I first came out."

Last October, a month after police
announced they would not be bringing
any charges against Hale after claims
he had embellished his account of

# Was this

events in B
Pity, he says
Wales. He
detective c
other possi
including v
serving life
presenter J

**HE** say
relieve
area,
couldn't ge

"If I wer
people wan
you move s
Bakewell, t

He is still
innocent.
police have
they haven'
of inquiry
or wrong. T

Referring
about Steph
said that M

OUT: Downing leaves
court a free man with
Don Hale in 2002

## [NEW]SPAPER CAMPAIGN MADE
## [RE]PORTRAYS HIM AS NAIVE
## [AND] HELPED CLEAR OF MURDER

TAKE 2: Tompkinson and Jason Watkins

IN 1973, Downing was interrogated for nine hours without caution and without a solicitor. He was shaken and his hair was pulled. All four factors were keys to the eventual overturning of his convictions.

He signed a confession but retracted it 15 days later, saying he believed Wendy would regain consciousness and identify the real attacker.

Five months later he was jailed for life on the basis of his confession and samples of Wendy's blood on his clothes.

Because he was "in denial of murder", he faced the prospect of life behind bars without any chance of parole until Hale took up his case.

**T**HE ex-editor says: "It wasn't just a question of Stephen's statement being wrong. I couldn't find any evidence to say that he had done it."

His early investigations uncovered discrepancies in scene-of-crime photographs. House-to-house inquiries uncovered witnesses who claimed they were turned away by police when they offered statements.

Sensationally, Hale revealed that Wendy had a love-child, putting paid to denials that she had been having an affair.

There were three reports of a blood-stained man seen fleeing the cemetery. But most significant of all was the terrified young schoolgirl Hale tracked down to a Greek Island 21 years after the murder, who said she had seen Wendy in the arms of a man in the cemetery that day.

"She still bears the identity of the man and she still thinks she could be killed for knowing it," says Hale.

He has the names of what he believes are five possible suspects and claims Wendy had two-long-term affairs and six possibly night, others.

He makes no apologies for what he calls his "muck-raking" of her love life.

"It was part of a quest for justice," he says. "She wasn't the Bakewell Tart, but she was a young woman who wasted a bit of fun.

"I may not be able to prove who killed Wendy Sewell, but I can prove Downing didn't. Downing couldn't have done it, but others could, were there and had motives. Nobody has bothered to look for them."

While the arguments continue to rage, it seems the truth about the Sewell murder will remain a mystery.

Even after playing Hale to Jason Watkins's Downing, Stephen Tompkinson wasn't sure what to believe.

People in Bakewell are still split 50/50," he says.

"There were people who believed that the police got the right man at the time and didn't see why their licence fee was being wasted by the BBC on giving publicity to this awful crime. And there were others who knew Stephen very well and didn't think he was capable of such a crime then.

"The closer you get to it, all you see are grey areas."

very naive. He spent 27 years in prison and came out almost as he was when he went in, aged 17. He hadn't developed mentally and was very childlike.

He should never have got involved with Christine. I knew she was trying to sell kiss-and-tell stories but he became obsessed with her. I've listened to the tapes. He never actually confesses to murder.

Of the law firm receptionist, he says: "He had been talking to [the girl] for some time and flirting with her. When she realised he was in jail for murder and sex offences, she panicked."

In Denial Of Murder presents Wendy's story as the backcloth to Hale's campaign to free Downing.

When last year's police inquiry cast doubt on Hale's investigations, the script he had written was scrapped and scriptwriter Neil McKay reworked it.

Stephen Tompkinson acted out the role of Hale on the streets of Bakewell last autumn and noticed Downing among the crowds who lined the pavements to watch him.

More ominous still was the disturbing thought that if Stephen didn't kill Wendy Sewell, the real murderer could also have been watching.

The 37-year-old actor was even approached by a local woman who mistook him for the real Hale. She told how she'd been turned away by police when she offered information at the time of the murder. On September

TAPES: Downing with clairvoyant Christine Smith

mirror/factory.mgn.co.uk

### ust[i]ce?

---

## Wendy Sewell (1973)
Stephen Downing was freed in February 2001 after serving 27 years for the murder of Wendy Sewell. His conviction was overturned, leaving the victim's family still waiting for justice.

LYNNE: She died in hospital from head injuries.

---

## Maniac alert as raped girl dies

By JACK McEACHRAN and RACHEL HEBDITCH

**P**RETTY teenager Lynne Weedon— victim of a sex maniac —died yesterday.

She was raped and battered in a dimly-lit alley near her home a week ago.

She died in hospital from head injuries.

Detectives fear that the vicious killer might strike again.

And last night Detective Chief Superintendent David Frew, who heads the murder hunt, appealed to women to help flush him out.

Mr. Frew said the police wanted to hear from anyone who knew of

a man who got home with blood-stained clothing last Wednesday night or Thursday morning.

The attack happened on Wednesday night near 16-year-old Lynne's home in Lampton Avenue, Hounslow, Middlesex.

She had vowed that she would never use the short-cut alleyway after dark because it was frequented by prowlers.

But Lynne did use the alley after a late night out with friends.

The killer dragged her

Continued on Page Two

---

### Eve Stratford (1975), and Lynne Weedon (1975)
Eve Stratford, pictured with fellow bunny girls and WBC light heavy[we]ight boxer John Conte[h] (left). Her 1975 case was reopened in 2007 following a breakthrough in DNA techniques that linked her murder to that of teenager Lynne Weedon (right). Both cases remain unsolved.

**Genette Tate (1978), and April Fabb (1969)** Genette Tate vanished while cycling in a Devon village. Moments after speaking to two school friends, her bike was found abandoned in a country lane. No trace of her has ever been found.

# RIDDLE AS A VILLAGE NEWSGIRL VANISHES

### By GEOFFREY LAKEMAN

A MASSIVE police hunt was going on last night for a village paper girl who cycled into thin air.

Tate, was last seen by two school chums she met during her afternoon round.

She chatted for a moment, then pedalled around the corner of a

LOST: Village newspaper girl Genette Tate

# GENETTE COPS TO QUIZ TRIPLE CHILD KILLER

**VICTIM**

**SO EVIL**

Dad hopes for answers on mystery

0800 056 7103

FOUND: Genette's bike abandoned in the road

## FRAN'S FREE FEA A YARD

Genette's parents have never given up hope of discovering what happened to their daughter. In April each year her father John makes a pilgrimage to the site of her disappearance, while mother Sheila arranged for a memorial stone to be erected in the village of Aylesbeare in 2011.

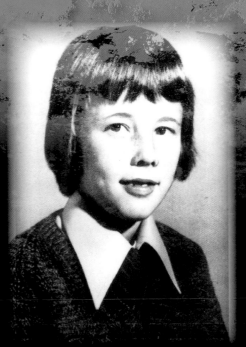

**Carl Bridgewater (1978)** Carl Bridgewater, a 13-year-old newspaper delivery boy, was shot when he disturbed raiders at a lonely farmhouse in Staffordshire in September 1978.

The scene of the crime: Yew Tree Farm. Carl was dragged or lured into the living room by robbers, who were systematically stripping the house of silver and antiques worth just over £100.

**Suzy Lamplugh (1986)** Forensic officers search an area in Pershore, Worcestershire, in August 2010 in an attempt to find the body of Suzy Lamplugh (inset), missing since 1986.

**Julie Ward (1988)** The remains of Julie Ward were discovered in a Kenyan safari park in 1988 but, despite vast amounts of money having been spent in tracking her killers, no one has yet been convicted of her murder.

# MOTORWAY REMAINS ARE MISSING MEL

## She vanished on night out 13 yrs ago

**Melanie Hall (1996)** Hospital worker Melanie Hall disappeared after a night out in 1996; her remains were found alongside the busy M5 near Thornbury 13 years later.

# 13 years ago we had a vibrant daughter. Now all we have left is a bag of bones
## MEL'S PARENTS TELL OF AGONY

**Billie-Jo Jenkins (1997)** Billie-Jo Jenkins was found brutally murdered at her foster family's home in Hastings in February 1997.

# BILLIE-JO HAD FOUND HOPE OF HAPPINESS AFTER A LIFE OF DESPAIR

**Jill Dando (1999)** Popular television presenter Jill Dando was shot on her doorstep in April 1999.

The scene outside Jill Dando's home (above) at 29 Gowan Avenue, Fulham, London, in the immediate aftermath of her shooting.

Former Manchester police chief John Stalker (right), pictured here beside a police Appeal for Assistance poster in a shop window, had his own theories regarding the murder of Jill Dando.

The people of her hometown turn out in force as Jill Dando is buried in Weston-super-Mare. Suspect Barry George (inset) arrives handcuffed at Bow Street Magistrates Court in March 2001. George was convicted of the murder of Jill Dando in July 2001 but was retried and eventually acquitted in August 2008.

**Brighton Trunk Murders (1934)** William Joseph Vinnicombe at the left luggage office of Brighton railway station on 17th June 1934. The cloakroom attendant became aware of a smell in the room and alerted the police. Chief Inspector Ronald Donaldson opened the trunk to find the dismembered torso of a woman.

Police search near Brighton racecourse in a vain attempt to solve the Brighton Trunk Murders of 1934.

**Jack the Stripper (1959–65)** Chief Inspector John du Rose was the detective in charge of the Jack the Stripper (aka Hammersmith murders) case 1964–1965, when a serial killer operating in London, killed between six and eight women prostitutes, dumping their bodies around London or in the River Thames.

Police surround an alley in Swyncombe Avenue, Brentford, where the body of Helene Barthelemy was found on 24th April 1964.

A police identikit of the two men who were last seen with Margaret McGowan at a Kensington car park in October 1964.

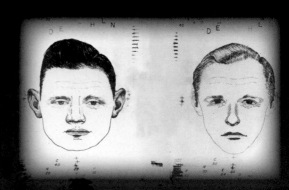

Some of Jack the Stripper's victims: Gwyneth Rees, Hannah Tailford, Irene Lockwood and Margaret McGowan.

**Bible John (1968–69)** Police enlist the public in an attempt to catch Bible John, a notorious murderer of women, operating in Glasgow in 1969.

## Another Tory cock-up

*Two girls found dead in wood*

# MURDER

**VICTIM: Karen**

**VICTIM: Nicola**

# HORROR

**TWO little girls allowed out to buy sweets were found brutally murdered yesterday.**

The bodies of Nicola Fellows, 10, and her nine-year-old playmate Karen Hadaway were discovered dumped under trees at a beauty spot called the "Wild Park.

The beast who attacked them strangled them with his bare hands.

But the helpless pals were not sexually assaulted.

Their pathetic little bodies lay side by side.

The callous killer had not even tried to conceal his hideous crime.

Officers immediately stepped up their hunt for a ginger-haired man in a blue car who has tried to abduct several young children in the area recently.

**By EDWARD VALE and TOM MERRIN**

A driver and car matching the description were spotted parked opposite the shop where the girls were last seen alive on Thursday evening.

Nicola and Karen had left their homes on the Moulsecoomb Estate in Brighton, to buy sweets at a nearby shop.

They changed their

▶ **Turn to Page 3**

## Strangler kills them with his bare hands

# OH NORMAN! Who's got his figures in a twist then?

**OH DEAR!** The Tories are in such a tizzy about the Mirror that they've cocked it up again.

After Norman Fowler, Tory chairman, had sounded off on Wednesday, Norman Tebbit, the party chairman, had another go yesterday.

The two Normans are upset by the Mirror's campaign against the Government's destruction of the National Health Service.

Read Mr Tebbit: "I tell Mr Maxwell (Robert Maxwell, publisher of the Mirror), if his circulation was so high he had no advertising on his paper the paper would be in a better state."

**FACT**
The circulation of the Mirror in September, 1986 was up 5.4 per cent over September, 1985 from 2,987,000 to 3,056,000.

**FACT**
The spending on NHS hospitals after allowing for inflation...

...over the past year is up by ONE HALF OF ONE PER CENT.

These are just more figures Norman Tebbit. They're the figures Norman Fowler gave to the National Association of Health Authorities.

Had Norman's spending gone up last year at the same rate as the Mirror's circulation, there would not be so much envy and hurtful waiting lists, so much anxiety, and so much hatred for the Government for what it has done to the NHS.

And then the two Normans wouldn't be cocking it up much like the Two Ronnies.

**Mirror circulation up over 5%**
**Hospital spending only ½%**

---

**Babes in the Wood Killings – Nicola Fellows and Karen Hadaway (1986)** The bodies of Nicola Fellows (10) and Karen Hadaway (9) were found in a beauty spot in East Sussex in October 1986. Despite the police's best efforts, the girls' killer has remained unpunished.

a report for review by the Home Office. When he wrote the 49-page report it cost him his job on a newspaper – but it was also eventually gave Michael Shirley his life back. The campaign was faced with many setbacks, including the time when the then home secretary, Michael Howard, refused to refer the case to the Court of Appeal, even though the circumstantial evidence at the original trial was flimsy at best. Then, in 2001 and 2002, Hampshire police "found" evidence that could be used in DNA testing, which would finally set Shirley free. In July 2003, Michael Shirley was freed after spending more than 16 years in prison for a crime he didn't commit. It was the first time in legal history that DNA evidence was brought into a case in order to prove that a convicted prisoner was not guilty of a crime.

Linda Cook's murderer was, and possibly is, still at large; he has never been brought to justice for the killing of a young woman who should have had the rest of her life in front of her.

# Elaine Doyle

(1986)

On 1st June 1986, 16-year-old Elaine Doyle went with three friends to a disco in Laird Street, Greenock. It was a good evening for all concerned and at around 8.30pm, as it was the first time she had been out for such an evening, Elaine telephoned her parents from the club to let them know that she would be home around 12.30am. After the disco, Elaine and her girlfriends sat outside the Mid Kirk in Cathcart Square, having bought food from a mobile hamburger van nearby. Although it was a Sunday night, the surrounding streets were busy as the following day was a bank holiday. Elaine left her friends just after 12.00am and began her journey home on foot. Her friend, Lynn Ryan, had offered to let Elaine stay at her house, but as the 16-year-old had already phoned her parents earlier in the evening to tell them she would be home, and as by this time it was too late for her to call again, she decided not to change her plans. Not far from the church, she bumped into two other friends in Hamilton Way, with whom she had a brief chat before wishing them goodnight and walking off alone.

The following morning at around 7.30am, Elaine's strangled body was discovered by a man on his way to work. She was partially clothed and lying in undergrowth near a lane in Ardgowan Street where she lived with her parents, Jack and Maureen. She was literally 50 yards from her home. Her blue handbag was the only missing item. The post-mortem confirmed strangulation with some kind of ligature, which was never found, and also pointed to the fact that the attack had a sexual motive. Elaine had been assaulted. The young girl had desperately fought her attacker, but police believe that she never stood a chance.

A week after the murder, the young victim's bag was spotted on fire outside on the steps leading up to the Watt Library. Police believed the stunt was aimed at taunting them. What it also told them was that the killer, or someone who knew the killer, was still in Greenock at least one week after the murder. They either lived there or had an extremely good knowledge of the area. Witnesses talked of a man in the area on the night of the murder who was acting suspiciously, but no one seemed to have a name for the suspect. Despite a thorough search for the killer and an extensive list of suspects, no one was brought to justice for the mindless attack on Elaine Doyle.

Many years went by and eventually the case was closed, unsolved. However, 17 years later, the case was reopened after a DNA breakthrough. It was 2003 when detectives, led by John Dearie, finally had the resources to build up a full DNA profile of the killer, and Elaine's parents – who were still in anguish over the death of their daughter – hoped that they could finally discover why their daughter had been murdered and by whom. The murderer, it was established, was aged between 16 and 34 at the time of the attack. However, nothing else came to light over the next eight years. Then, in July 2011, the BBC programme *Crimewatch* covered the case during the 25th anniversary year of the murder and more than 140 calls (50 of them to the show) were received as a result. One name was given to police twice by different callers and a total of 70 names in all looked like strong leads.

The cold case team from Strathclyde police contacted colleagues in New South Wales and Queensland, Australia, in order to trace the six possible suspects on the other side of the globe. Meanwhile, a further 64 people were also being investigated. Two men in Switzerland were eventually eliminated from inquiries once their DNA was tested and found not to match that of swabs taken from the crime scene. A combined press appeal also gave rise to possible suspects, and some who had already been eliminated during the original investigation found themselves back on the list. The DNA database in Britain and Europe was also searched for possible matches and police were confident that the murderer would be caught out by the technology. Although police recognized that the killer could possibly be dead in 2011, they believed they were looking for someone in their 40s or 50s and felt that it was likely that they could find the perpetrator unless that person had met an untimely death. No other suspects were found to be connected at the time.

Jack Doyle made a number of emotional appeals for anyone with information about his daughter's death to come forward. He described how he and his wife and family could take some comfort from just knowing why their daughter had been killed and by whom. The family needed to make sense of the vicious crime that had been carried out on their loved one and found no peace in not knowing what happened to Elaine. Like many people who lose a family member to a violent unsolved crime, the Doyles were looking for answers to help make their lives just a little more bearable. As in all these cases, the likelihood is that someone, somewhere, even if they are not the killer, knows facts that could aid the police and bring some rest for the victim's family.

# Julie Ward

(1988)

Established in 1948 as a wildlife sanctuary, for many the Masai Mara National Reserve in southwest Kenya, with its breathtaking backdrop and stunning animals, is a haven for amazing holidays and safaris. It's home to zebra, the Thomson's gazelle, wildebeest and game, and has an exceptional population of big cats. However, for 28-year-old publishing assistant Julie Ward, who was on a photography safari, it became a deathtrap. Julie went missing in September 1988 and her dismembered body was found a week later. There was evidence that the body had also been burned and, to begin with, Kenyan officials stated that the victim had been mauled by a wild cat and then struck by lightning. However, John Ward, Julie's father, who had flown out from his home in Bury St Edmunds in Suffolk to Kenya to help search for her when she went missing, found that she had not fallen prey to a lion, but had in fact been hacked to death and burned in an attempt to cover up what had happened. The only remains of his daughter found initially were her left leg and jawbone. When he was met with failure to recognize that she had been murdered he launched his own investigation into what had happened.

Ward also discovered that the coroner's report had been altered to try and cover up the fact that Julie's bones had been cut by an extremely sharp blade and not gnawed by wild animals. Her father's investigation led to an inquest which began on 9th August 1989.

When her last moments were revealed for the first time at the Nairobi hearing, evidence was presented to suggest that Julie may have had her leg hacked off as she fled for her life on the game safari park – the pathologist explained that the calf muscle in the leg was in the posture of someone running. Paul Weld-Dixon, a friend, was called to try and identify the remains and was told by the pathologist that the body parts had been severed with a sharp instrument, instantly making the case one of a murder. Just one day after the inquest began, safari park worker David Nchoka was dramatically accused of killing the British heiress, but he wasn't the only suspect that police were investigating. Nchoka was visibly shaking in court as he struggled to answer questions about what had happened to Julie, who went missing near Keekorok Lodge, where she'd been staying, after her jeep got stuck in a gully.

Businessman John Ward had hired helicopters and Land Rovers when he first arrived in Kenya in a bid to find his missing daughter. Following the discovery of the victim's left leg and jawbone, further bones, a charred skull and a mass of ash were found. Julie's father collected the ash and bones from the red dust with his bare hands before placing them in a bag and taking them to Nairobi. The pathologist at the time made it fairly clear to Mr Ward that he believed the young British woman had been murdered but, later, a British diplomat in Kenya who read the pathologist's report was convinced that the phrase "clean cut" had been altered to "torn". Fearing that the death of a beautiful British subject on Kenyan soil would be ruinous for the country's tourist industry, it was believed that the police tried to blame the horrendous crime on the safari's wildlife. On 11th August 1989, a Kenyan policeman responsible for security at the game park, Jerald Karori, was the second man accused of murder. By September 1989, the whole world was given the news that the victim's head had been cut off by a single blow from behind, according to a top pathologist Professor Austin Gresham. The inquest ended in triumph for wealthy hotel owner John Ward when a Kenyan magistrate agreed with him and recorded a verdict of murder on 27th October 1989. Julie's father had been on a one-man crusade and now a massive hunt for Julie's killers could begin. At this point, the investigation had cost John Ward £100,000. He also had a prime suspect in mind, game park warden Simon Makallah, who had never been charged by police.

In November 1989, a British holidaymaker became the key figure in the unsolved murder when Ward received an anonymous letter from Blackpool claiming that the author knew the identity of the killer. However, it was pointed out that the letter could have been written in Kenya and sent back with a tourist to be posted in Britain. The letter gave a first name for the alleged killer, but no surname. While the name was not one previously linked to the investigation, the letter did provide some unusual information, which led John Ward to believe that it was genuine. The letter was passed to a private detective working for the hotel owner. The investigation led to two gamekeepers being arrested on 14th March the following year. Scotland Yard detectives, who flew to Kenya, questioned the men about the murder, having sifted through all the evidence. Detective Superintendent Graham Searle and Inspector Dave Shipperlee quickly made their dramatic arrests of Peter Kipeen (26) and Jonah Magiroi (28), after Kenya's President Moi made a personal plea to then Foreign Secretary Douglas Hurd for help in solving the case.

By 1992, John Ward had made 25 trips to Kenya and had spent around £300,000 trying to trace his daughter's killers. He was to face the two suspects in court for the first time in February that year, where he hoped they would be found guilty. However, Janet Ward, Julie's mother, was determined that should the two men be found guilty that they should not hang. She told the press: "The thought of these two men hanging is abhorrent. But if I thought they were guilty, so is the thought of them getting off." She further added: "I only want to know the truth."

On 10th February 1992, a court heard how the two men had tried to "wipe her [Julie] off the face of the earth". It was alleged that before Kipeen and Magiroi hacked the young woman to death and tried to burn the remains of her body, they held her captive for six days. The trial also heard how Julie had been decapitated with one fell swipe while her head was bowed. During the trial, defence lawyer James Orengo claimed that a policeman and a game park gatekeeper (named as Karori and Nchoko) were actually responsible for the murder, and that Julie Ward had been the victim of a six-day sex ordeal carried out by them. However, the police believed there was no evidence against these two men, and the proceedings continued. All four men maintained their innocence.

Later that month, the safari park became notorious for a spate of rapes and robberies, and tourists were warned to stay away from it. In one of the worst incidents, two German couples were robbed by armed bandits who then battered one of the men and forced him to watch them rape his pregnant wife.

At the end of June, both Kipeen and Magiroi walked free amid accusations that the inquiry had been one giant bungle by the Kenyan police. Giving his verdict, Judge Fidahussein Abdullah also slammed the Scotland Yard detectives for "browbeating" the two men and went on to accuse three prosecution witnesses – Makallah, Nchoko and Karori – of "knowing more than they care to tell" about the murder.

More than a year later, in December 1993, an eyewitness, who was a former chauffeur to a politician, came forward with claims that Julie Ward had stumbled across a gang of gun and drug smugglers and that he had witnessed the murder of the young heiress. He described her death in detail to John Ward after defecting from his former employer, and gave in-depth accounts of the crimes that he had witnessed during his employment. John Ward spoke with the new witness for 75 minutes at a secret location in Nairobi; he told the victim's father that his daughter had been silenced after she came across the men. Mr Ward stated in the press: "I am not prepared to reveal at this stage what he said, but his detailed account corroborates many previous pieces of information I had received. He was able to describe the scene of the murder in detail and give a full and accurate description of Julie." John Ward wanted to talk with the man again but, on the following day, police raided the house before he could do so and the man fled. The driver did get in touch with John Ward again and it was known that he was one of four witnesses to the murder.

Ten years later, Simon Makallah was arrested and charged with Julie's murder to her family's great relief. In May, 11 years after the killing, Makallah had still not been found guilty and the case made legal history when it was moved to Britain at Kenya's High Commission in London on 12th May 1999. By 17th September it was all over and Makallah was the third man to be cleared of the murder. For John Ward it was a devastating blow; he had devoted his life and spent more than £500,000 in the search for the truth.

Ward hoped in January 2003 that a change of government in Kenya headed by Mwai Kibaki would see the case reopened. In April 2004 a British inquest into the case did open, at which John Ward gave evidence. Choking back tears, Ward described how he saw Julie's severed left leg, jawbone and a pile of ashes where she had been burned. By now, he had spent a staggering £1 million trying to get to the truth. Then, in April 2004, the Kenyan government admitted that there had been a cover-up with regard to the death of the publishing assistant. The news came on the third day of a new inquest, and new witnesses began to come forward, no longer afraid of reprisals due to the new government being in place. It was hoped that any new evidence would also be aided by new forensic science techniques. But nothing new was discovered, and the Ward family were still no nearer claiming justice. Hopes were raised again in May 2008 when a credible witness came forward who was willing to testify that he saw Julie with her suspected killer on the day she was murdered. John Ward also had 10 new leads and was closer than he had ever been to getting to the truth. But, nearly four years later, no killer has yet been convicted of Julie's murder and the case continues.

# Sandy Drummond

(1991)

When the body of 33-year-old Sandy Drummond was found on a farm track on 24th June 1991 in Boarhills, Fife, the initial findings of the forensic team were that he had died of natural causes. Drummond, a quiet self-contained man, lived in an isolated cottage near St Andrews, which he shared with his brother Jimmy. He had worked at the Guardbridge Paper Mill for seven years, but he never socialized with colleagues. In fact, when Sandy Drummond died, many of his colleagues at the paper mill didn't even know who he was. His hobbies were solitary and he kept himself to himself.

When it was discovered after further investigation of the body that Sandy had injuries to his neck, police began a murder inquiry, which sparked more questions than it answered. As Sandy was known to be a creature of habit, once police began probing into the events surrounding the death of the Scotsman, they discovered that a number of things had occurred which were potentially quite out of character. First, Drummond had withdrawn several sums of money – amounting to more than £700 – from his bank account. (Most of this was subsequently found in the brothers' cottage after Sandy's death.) He died on a Monday but had, mysteriously, rung his employer on the Friday before to hand in his notice, refusing to work his notice period of one week. He didn't tell his brother Jimmy that he had resigned until the Sunday evening before his death. Sandy Drummond didn't particularly go into any detail with his brother, but he did mention that he was in need of a break from his usual routine and that he was thinking of going away on his bike for a while.

On Monday 24th June, Jimmy Drummond left for work as usual. Within minutes, Sandy was spotted running out of the cottage with a blue sports bag which he carried across the road to the fields opposite. The blue bag was never found during the police investigation and, stranger still, an orange Morris Marina was parked outside the isolated cottage on two occasions during the day. The car was never traced and neither was its owner so police have no idea who visited Sandy Drummond or even whether the driver of the vehicle had anything to do with his tragic death. Equally intriguing was the fact that a strange man with a bloodstained bandage wrapped around his hand – who remains unidentified – caught a bus at 2.30pm near the cottage on the day of the killing. With the victim having led a solitary existence and the isolated location of the cottage, police had very little to go on in their quest to find Sandy's killer. There were two reconstructions of the crime on television but no significant information was gleaned from viewers.

The case remains the only unsolved murder inquiry in Fife and police are keen to stress that any new evidence will be investigated thoroughly.

# Lindsay Jo Rimer

(1994)

Lindsay Jo Rimer was just 13 years old when she went missing on 7th November 1994. The Calder High School student was a popular girl who lived with her parents, brother and two sisters on Cambridge Street, in Hebden Bridge, West Yorkshire.

At about 10.00pm on the day she went missing, Lindsay left home to walk to the small local supermarket on Crown Street to buy a packet of cornflakes. Knowing that her mother was out having a drink with a friend, she stopped off at the Trades Club in Holme Street to say hello. The young teenager was invited to stay for a glass of coke, but she declined and continued on her journey towards the shop. Rimer bought the box of cereal at 10.22pm – which was caught on CCTV cameras – but this was to be the last time she would be seen alive. Rimer didn't return home that night, but she wasn't missed until the following morning when she didn't turn up for her paper round. When the alarm was raised, police were initially inclined to think that the young girl had run away. Although her family denied it, there was speculation and rumour that she had been having trouble at home. Despite a reconstruction of the events surrounding Rimer's disappearance and her final walk to the local supermarket, no trace of Lindsay was found for several months.

It was not until 12th April 1995 that the body of the 13-year-old was eventually found by two workmen, weighted down in the Rochdale

Canal about a mile away from her home. While the pathologist, Professor Mike Green, suspected that the victim had been strangled due to the fact that her voice box had been flattened against her spinal column, he concluded that the attack had not been of a sexual nature. No real clues presented themselves immediately prior to the discovery of the body but, in the intervening years, literally hundreds of statements from witnesses were taken and the police spoke to more than 5,000 people throughout the investigation. In addition, known violent criminals were investigated, but no evidence was found to connect these people with Lindsay Jo Rimer's death.

In 2011, a new appeal was launched to try and find the missing answers to the mystery surrounding the killing of the young girl. It was 17 years since she had first gone missing but police were convinced that somebody must have vital information. They urged anyone with any knowledge of what had happened to the teenager to come forward and help them solve the crime.

# Melanie Hall

(1996)

Hospital clerical worker Melanie Hall simply disappeared from a nightclub on 9th June 1996. The 25-year-old had spent the evening with doctor boyfriend Phil Kurlbaum and a couple of friends at Cadillac's nightclub in Bath and continued dancing with her two companions after Phil left at around 1.00am because he was feeling unwell. That same night, just hours before the blonde-haired victim went missing, Linda Hamblin – aged 42 from Cardiff – was threatened just a few hundred yards from the club. Describing the attack, Hamblin said that she was threatened by a man wielding a knife who said he would cut her throat if she screamed. The man tried to push her into a car but, despite being badly cut, she managed to escape her attacker.

Melanie Hall was supposed to be staying with her German boyfriend that night, but it was alleged that the couple had had a minor row prior to him leaving the club. As her parents were not expecting their daughter to come home to Bradford on Avon, the alarm was not raised until 11th June 1996 when she failed to turn up to work. After Melanie disappeared, police carried out a number of searches of the River Avon and began interviewing hundreds of clubbers and taxi drivers in an attempt to find the missing University of Bath graduate. Even a £10,000 reward for information and two television programmes highlighting the case failed to bring forth any evidence.

On 25th September 1996, Melanie's mother Patricia Hall had an open letter published in the press appealing for help from the public. In it she wrote: "I know that as days turn to weeks and weeks to months, fears for her safety grow ... Melanie is such a kind thoughtful girl." She went on to write: "Since her disappearance the house seems so quiet. The music and laughter have gone."

Patricia Hall pleaded with the British public to come forward if they had any information that might shed light on the case, no matter how insignificant they thought it might be. She said that if her daughter were alive she hoped she was safe and well. Mrs Hall also asked, should her daughter be dead, for the chance to bring her body home so that she could be laid to rest. It was a moving letter which concluded with her thoughts for other families grieving for the loss of a loved one and hoping that they could find strength to face the future, whatever that might be.

Convicted killer of newly wed Shirley Banks and prime suspect in the Suzy Lamplugh case, John Cannan, was questioned over the disappearance of Melanie in 1998. Known for his Bristol connections, Cannan became of interest to police when allegations that he plotted the murder of Hall from his prison cell came to light. Officers were told that Cannan – who was 44 at the time – and another inmate in Durham jail spent long hours planning the "perfect" abduction. It was alleged that Cannan's accomplice was a convicted rapist who put the plan into action after being released from prison. Melanie Hall was chosen as the random victim. Melanie's parents feared that if Cannan was responsible for planning the abduction and murder of their daughter then they would never know the truth about what happened to her; the convicted killer was renowned for believing that knowledge was power. Cannan's solicitor strongly denied the allegations.

By August 1998, rapist Christopher Clark had become the prime suspect in the case. He was interviewed by police about the attack while in jail, and was suspected because, just two months before Melanie went missing, Clark had been freed early from a 14-year sentence for a string of sex assaults. Clark had been questioned by police at the time the victim vanished, but he denied his involvement, gave an alibi and was released. However, Clark attacked a young teacher in Bath a month after Melanie Hall disappeared. The woman fought him off and he was convicted of the attack when he was trapped by DNA bloodspots which he left on her clothes. He was given a life sentence at Bristol Crown Court in August 1997. Clark allegedly hatched the plan to abduct and murder a victim while he was serving an earlier sentence in the same jail as Cannan in the early 1990s. Clark also happened to have been in the Bath area at the time Melanie went missing and it was believed by police that he was quite possibly the man they were looking for. Clark had a dark criminal past and had raped several victims, including schoolgirls and housewives; he was described as a severe threat to women. By this time, the police and Melanie's family believed her to be dead, but Clark was not charged with her murder.

A year later, a new witness came forward to describe that they had seen a man and a woman arguing on the riverbank on the night Melanie Hall disappeared. The police launched a search of the River Avon between Cleveland Bridge and Chatham Row in Bath following the BBC's *Crimewatch* programme, which highlighted the three-year investigation. However, no evidence of Melanie was found in the river and it would be another year before more leads came to light. The killer of student Rebecca Storrs was quizzed over Melanie in December 2000. Marc Shillibier had just been jailed for the brutal murder of Storrs, who was strangled and mutilated, and the fact that he was jailed in Cardiff led police to believe he could have been in the Bath area at the right time. This line of inquiry also came to nothing but, on 12th March 2003, two men in their 30s were held by police. The men were both later released. In 2004, Avon coroner Paul Forrest was asked to hold an inquest in order to rule that Melanie could be declared dead despite the fact that her body had never been found. Forrest was forced to record an open verdict due to lack of evidence, but did speculate that Melanie had probably been killed not long after she went missing.

Melanie's remains were eventually found in a bin liner beside the M5 motorway in August 2009. The black bag – containing her skull, pelvis, leg and arm bones – was found by a workman by the northbound slip road of junction 14 near Thornbury. Although Melanie's parents spoke of their sense of relief at finally knowing what had happened to their daughter, they also told of the agony they had been through and the untold anguish that they felt. Forensic experts searched the scene while tests were carried out to determine how Melanie died. The tests showed that Melanie had been beaten with a blunt weapon, which fractured her skull, cheek and jaw before she died. She was then wrapped in bin bags and bound with rope.

In October 2009, keys found on the motorway verge not far from where Melanie's body was found led police to believe that they could be linked to her killer. The Ford car keys dated back to the year that Melanie went missing, but, as with all other lines of inquiry, the find did not bring the killer to justice. Melanie Hall was buried on 11th December 2009 in a funeral service attended by more than 1,200 mourners and her heartbroken family, who were still no closer to discovering who was responsible for her death.

# Billie-Jo Jenkins

(1997)

When Bill Jenkins was imprisoned and the mother of his daughter could no longer cope on her own at their home in east London, their nine-year-old child was placed in foster care. Billie-Jo Jenkins was sent to live with Siôn and Lois Jenkins – who, despite the same surname, were not related to her – in Hastings, East Sussex. On 15th February 1997, at the age of 13, she was found brutally murdered at her foster parents' home. She had been battered to death with an iron tent peg, which her murderer had used to rain down on her skull more than 10 vicious blows. When Siôn Jenkins returned home with daughters Annie and Charlotte he is alleged to have found Billie-Jo on the patio covered and surrounded by blood. But tragedy soon turned to allegations when Jenkins was suspected by police of murdering his foster daughter after blood spots were found on his clothing. But there were also other suspects in the frame at the time. A man with mental health issues was eliminated from enquiries and another man, who was smartly dressed, was seen near to the house soon after the attack took place; however, he wasn't covered in blood. Police were confident of Jenkins' guilt and even told Lois Jenkins that they believed they had the murderer, despite the fact that Charlotte mentioned while being questioned that the side gate to the rear of the property might have been open when they returned home from shopping. Jenkins was charged with murder even though he protested vehemently that he was completely innocent of the crime.

In 1998, Siôn Jenkins was convicted of the murder of Billie-Jo and Lois divorced him, moving their daughters with her to Tasmania. She severed all contact with her former husband. During the trial it transpired that Siôn Jenkins was a liar who had faked his CV in order to gain a deputy headship at a local school in Hastings, but he went on to declare that he had been stupid to make the false claims. He began serving his prison sentence for the murder of the young teenager who had been entrusted to his care but appealed in 1999. It failed, but a second appeal in 2004 found his conviction unsafe and it was quashed. He was released on bail pending a retrial. In fact, Jenkins was retried twice for the murder of Billie-Jo. The first retrial heard how the spots on Jenkins' clothes could have come from Billie-Jo's airway as he desperately tried to save her life when he found her dying on the patio on returning from a DIY store. The jury was unable to reach a majority verdict and Jenkins faced a second retrial. This too ended with the jury unable to come to a majority verdict, although crucial new evidence about the blood spots had come to light. It was found that within the microscopic blood spots, nine of the 148 spots had fragments of Billie-Jo's bone. The find, after analysis by Dr Jeremy Skepper from Cambridge University, came far too late as far as the trial judge was concerned and the jury was never informed of the new information. In February 2006 Jenkins was officially acquitted of murder.

It was around this time that first wife Lois – Jenkins had secretly wed a millionaire art dealer in early 2005 – made public the news that her former husband had been a cruel man with a history of domestic violence and mood swings. This evidence had, in fact, been given at one of his appeal hearings, although it had not been divulged to the jury. Like the murder, Jenkins denied the violence. He tried for £500,000 in damages for the six years he spent in prison, but this was rejected by the Ministry of Justice due to rules stating that compensation was only made for miscarriages of justice where the individual concerned was clearly innocent.

Billie-Jo's family were angry by the judge's decision to deny the evidence over the bone fragments found within the blood spots, which would probably have seen Jenkins convicted for a second time of the murder of the teenage girl. The jury was also unaware that Jenkins had a violent temper and often took his mood swings out on his entire family. At one point, it is alleged that Jenkins kicked Billie-Jo on her ankle, which she had sprained.

For the police it was back to square one when Jenkins was formally acquitted of the crime, but no new leads have ever been found. The case will, however, be reopened should new evidence be discovered and Billie-Jo's vicious killer will hopefully be brought to justice.

# Jill Dando

(1999)

The news that journalist, newsreader and television presenter Jill Dando had been shot dead outside her west London home on 26th April 1999 shocked the nation. Television and newspaper reports described how her dying screams echoed along a quiet street in Fulham as her assassin struck. TV's golden girl lay dead at the height of her glittering career. As police launched a massive hunt for the ruthless gunman, Queen Elizabeth II and Prime Minister Tony Blair led tributes to the BBC's *Crimewatch* presenter. Thirty-seven-year-old Jill was one of the BBC's highest paid stars, although she had been plagued by stalkers in the months before she died. She had spoken of fears for her own safety.

Detectives did not rule out the possibility that she was the victim of a crazed stalker although, equally, they considered whether she had disturbed an intruder in her home. Shocked neighbours told of her last terrifying moments as she lay dying from a single shot to the head on the doorstep of her £400,000 home. One of these was financial trader Richard Hughes (32), who was upstairs at his house in Gowan Avenue, Fulham, when he heard Jill setting the alarm on her BMW car, which was parked outside her terraced house, at around 11.30am. About 30 to 40 seconds later he heard the TV presenter scream for around five seconds. Running to the window, Hughes saw a man walking briskly away. He quickly went downstairs and made his way to the dying woman. Jill was lying on her doorstep, covered in blood and unconscious. To Hughes, Jill Dando didn't seem to be breathing. He couldn't find a pulse and described how she was already turning blue. He was joined by two other neighbours, one of whom went to call an ambulance. Jill was still clutching her car keys.

The first 999 call was received at 11.44am and two ambulance crews arrived within minutes, followed by two doctors in a fast-response car, while an air ambulance touched down in a school playground close by. Jill was treated at the scene before one of the ambulances transported her in a three-minute dash to Charing Cross Hospital, where a six-strong emergency team fought for 33 minutes to save her life. However, her brain injuries were just too severe and Jill Dando was confirmed dead at 1.03pm. Her death was announced just moments later by colleagues in the BBC newsroom. Her fiancé, consultant gynaecologist Alan Farthing, was off work that week because the couple were arranging the final preparations for their wedding, due to take place in September. Instead of organizing place settings, Farthing had the unenviable task of identifying Jill's body in the mortuary.

When police first arrived at the crime scene, they were unable to recognize the victim, as the head injury was so extensive, and they could not immediately tell if she had been stabbed or shot. Detectives believed that the killer had watched as Jill got out of her car, and had attacked her as she searched for her house keys. One of the first events following the murder saw police check security camera footage, as they tried to piece together the victim's last movements. (Jill had phoned the office of her agent, Jon Roseman, at around 10.20am that morning before heading to Ryman's stationers in King Street, Fulham, where she needed to buy an ink cartridge for her home printer.) The victim's blue BMW was also removed from Gowan Avenue, so that it could be forensically examined, and a hunt for the murder weapon got under way on a nearby stretch of the Thames. The police were initially looking for the body of a man who was said to have thrown himself off Putney Bridge shortly after the murder, but a spokesman confirmed not long after that the search had been narrowed down and that their main aim was to find the gun.

Jill Dando was pictured on the front of the *Radio Times* the week she was murdered, and colleagues paid tribute to her in a moving piece on their news programme. Martyn Lewis told viewers: "Jill was special not only to the millions of you who watched, admired and loved her over the years but to all of us who had the privilege and delight of working with her. The news was best when it was read by Jill. None of us could ever have believed it would one day be about her."

Distraught Alan Farthing told of his grief at the time of the murder, saying in a statement: "I am totally devastated and unable to comprehend what has happened. Jill was respected for her professional abilities, admired by all who met her and adored by anyone who got to know her." Her brother, journalist Nigel Dando, was working in the newsroom of the *Bristol Evening Post* when a couple of calls confirmed that his sister had been involved in an incident. He was given the news she had died by a newsflash on a TV in the office. Even John Hole (62) – who had put Jill through a four-year terrifying stalking ordeal – was shocked at the news of her death. The retired civil servant hadn't stalked the TV presenter for well over a year when she was killed, but found his house surrounded by reporters when he returned from a bike ride after the news was released. On Tuesday 27th April 1999, a description of the man that the police were looking for was released. He was white, five foot 11 inches tall, with dark hair, and aged between 30 and 40. He was thickset but well-groomed, and was wearing a Barbour-style jacket and carrying a mobile phone. Neighbours of Jill had been able to give police a detailed description of him as he fled the scene, but the question on everybody's minds was: who wanted Jill Dando dead?

Detective Chief Inspector Hamish Campbell, who was leading the investigation, asked the BBC for a list of all the crimes that Jill had reported on as a *Crimewatch* presenter, hoping it would provide clues to her killer, as the programme had featured a number of gangster-type shootings in recent years. Police also checked a list of prisoners released from jail in the preceding months who had been detained because of successful *Crimewatch* appeals. The police were, however, quick to point out that Jill only presented the programme; she had played no part in arresting or jailing criminals so a link to the TV programme – if there was one – was bizarre.

As Jill Dando was shot in the face at point-blank range with a 9mm pistol, police were mindful that they could be dealing with a professional assassin; the method of killing seemed to point to a man who had killed before, possibly several times. One Scotland Yard source said: "It takes a lot to walk up to a woman, look her in the eye and then blow her head apart with a bullet in the face." Officers from the National

Crime Squad, the National Criminal Intelligence Service and Scotland Yard studied the description of the gunman to see if he fitted any of the 20 or so contract killers known to have been operating in London or the south of the country at the time of the murder. It was known that some of these were underworld characters with established careers in armed robbery, drug smuggling and other organized crime. Other known gunmen were former soldiers, including Marines, who had worked as mercenaries or who had developed gangland connections. Jill had long been aware of the risks associated with presenting *Crimewatch*, and before taking the job had asked current and previous presenters if they had ever been threatened. Taking the job had made her more aware than ever of her personal safety.

In 1999, statistics showed that nearly 60 people in Britain were shot dead by hired hitmen. Assassins could be hired for as little as £1,000 in London, while in Liverpool and Manchester perpetrators as young as 16 could be hired for a few hundred pounds. Gangsters, drug barons and terrorists were the usual victims of hired guns, but police were well aware that husbands and wives could – either through jealousy or to gain life insurance – also hire an assassin. Police confirmed that it was known that in the few years prior to the murder, professionals from Ulster had been imported for gangland executions, and that it had become frighteningly easy to hire one of the millions of illegally owned guns. If Jill was killed by an assassin, then her killer had no direct link to her and was easily able to "melt away". There is never a direct link to the murder victim when a hitman strikes, and the tools of the trade are plucked easily and without trace from Britain's deadly arsenal of 4 million illegal guns. There is no incriminating paper trail and tracking down a lone hired killer is a nightmare for even the best investigating officer and their team. The chilling evidence in the Jill Dando case seemed to point to a contract killing.

As police pieced together the events of 26th April 1999, it was believed that the gunman lay in wait for his victim for an hour before he struck. There were seven sightings of the prime suspect, and police issued an urgent appeal for more witnesses to come forward. The first witness – a window cleaner – saw a man of the same description given by other witnesses carrying a mobile near Jill's house in Gowan Avenue at about 10.30am. Witness two, who was at the corner of Gowan Avenue and Munster Road, saw a smartly dressed man loitering near a disued building at around 11.30am. Witnesses three and four – Jill's next-door neighbour Hughes and a woman – saw the suspect seconds after the shooting at 11.35am. The man was jogging along Gowan Avenue towards Fulham Palace Road. Then, 20 minutes later, witnesses five and six saw the man near Putney Bridge, clambering over railings by the Thames. The last witness, waiting for a bus, provided the final clue to the murder when, a few minutes after the Putney Bridge sighting, the man emerged from Bishop's Park, which stretches down to the Thames, and ran along Fulham Palace Road. He waited at the bus stop and stood close enough for the witness to notice that he was sweating and had a mark on the bridge of his nose as if he had recently removed a pair of glasses. Police needed to ascertain whether these witnesses had seen different men – who all needed to be eliminated from the inquiry – or whether they had, in fact, all seen the same man. The gun used was believed to have been a Browning or a Tanfoglio, both of which had been banned in Britain following the Dunblane massacre (March 1996) in which 16 children and one adult were murdered following an attack at a school.

Staff at Ryman's in Hammersmith were among the last people to see Jill alive, and the thought that a hitman had been stalking the tree-lined streets of Fulham was horrifying to local residents. Two days after the murder, police were following up four theories, which included the presenter's private life, her work, politics and the possibility of a random attack. With regard to Jill's private life, police began questioning her previous lovers and those who knew her well in an attempt to find a clue as to why she was killed. Her fiancé's background was looked into to see if Jill's death was linked to someone from his past and police also investigated to see if the killing was the work of an obsessed fan who was in love with the presenter. Obviously, *Crimewatch* cases were looked at to establish if there was a link between the murder and Jill's work, which had covered nearly 500 crimes in the time since she had become a presenter in 1995. A revenge killing needed to be ruled out. The victim had also presented the BBC appeal for Kosovo refugees earlier in April 1999, and police pursued the possibility her killing was a political assassination. The appeal had helped raise more than £10 million, and Jill's death came just days after NATO blitzed Serbian TV in Belgrade, killing several employees. If this type of attack was to turn out to be in revenge, it would not have been the first time that BBC employees had suffered as a result of political executions. In 1975, World Service reporter Georgi Markov was stabbed with a poison pellet and, in 1994, World Service journalist Alison Ponting was targeted by a gunman who shot dead her sister, Karen Reed, by mistake, with the same type of gun and bullets that were used to kill Jill Dando.

The fourth possibility was that the TV presenter was the victim of a random killing by a crazed stalker or mental patient. But, just three days after the murder, 48-year-old BBC executive Tony Hall had to be moved from his home with his wife and two children and placed under 24-hour armed police guard for his safety when a Serb terror group claimed that it killed Jill Dando. The sensational development came after a male caller claiming to represent the group rang the BBC to say that Tony Hall was next. Security at BBC headquarters in London's Shepherd's Bush and in the West End was stepped up and a computerized E-fit of the man police were looking for was put together and was due to be released to the public on 1st May 1999. At the same time, police released the information that they were hunting for a blue Range Rover seen hurtling away from the area where the presenter was shot, after a tip-off received by the *Mirror*. By this time, police were sure that the murder was a contract killing carried out by two men. The metallic blue Range Rover was seen speeding down Doneraile Street, Fulham, directly opposite Gowan Avenue, on the day of the murder. It swerved right into Fulham Palace Road, ignoring a red light at a pedestrian crossing, before cutting in front of a white van and speeding off in the direction of Putney Bridge. Although it was caught on CCTV, the picture wasn't good enough to show the registration; however, police believed the vehicle to be either a back-up vehicle or getaway car for the gunmen. Former BBC war reporter Martin Bell was the next high-profile personality to receive a death threat, at the beginning of May. This was followed by threats to BBC journalist John Humphrys and BBC director of TV Alan Yentob. Meanwhile, the case continued.

In the first week of May 1999, police suspected that the killer had fled Britain immediately following the attack, and staff at Heathrow, Gatwick, Stansted and City airports were shown the E-fit of the man to see if anyone recognized him. At the end of the month, a *Crimewatch* appeal brought forward two more witnesses, one of whom saw the man believed to be the gunman on the number 74 bus, heading down Fulham Palace Road on the day of the shooting. What was hampering the investigation was the fact that there was little evidence of who the killer was. There was no DNA, no fingerprints, no contact with anyone, and no motive. However, he did leave behind a series of vital clues, including the murder weapon, the accomplices (as it became more and more clear that more than one man was involved), the blue Range Rover and the fact that Jill was killed on her own doorstep; how did the killer know she would be coming home that morning? Another clue was the bus stop on Fulham Palace Road. Did the killer really want to catch a bus or was he waiting for the Range Rover to pick him up and just chose the bus stop to wait at because it looked less suspicious? It was later assumed that the suspect did in fact take the 74 bus and probably met with his accomplice (in the blue Range Rover) at Putney Bridge.

John Stalker, former deputy chief constable of Greater Manchester police, had his own theories about the case. He didn't think that a spurned lover (following the announcement of Jill's engagement) would go to the trouble of hiring a team of three men at an estimated cost of £30,000 to end her life. This idea seemed, after four weeks of investigations, to be the route the police were following. While Stalker wasn't ruling this out, he concluded in a report for the *Daily Mirror* that Jill's killing bore all the hallmarks of a professional hit team and thus was more likely to be politically motivated. He also believed that an obsessive fan would be unlikely to shoot the victim in the face. He discussed the possibility that Jill was murdered in a case of mistaken identity – which investigating police had already ruled out. Stalker also felt that while criminals would probably blame a judge for sending them to prison, he felt it was extremely unlikely that they would blame the person fronting a TV show. He also thought that the fact the murder took place so soon after the killings in Belgrade had a significant part to play in the investigation.

By the end of May 1999, police had arrested funeral director James Shackleton for the murder. He was released without charge – despite the fact that he closely resembled the E-fit of the man described by witnesses – and it was reported in the press that Shackleton was not the prime suspect. Shackleton had been in the Fulham area on 26th April collecting wood for coffins for his low-cost funerals for the poor. Then, in June, police became convinced that Jill Dando had known her attacker and Hamish Campbell told Home Secretary Jack Straw that the murder was being treated as a "domestic". The police had, by this time, moved away from the train of thought that believed the murder was a Serb revenge killing or committed by a contract killer. The move towards the motive being a domestic affair came after the discovery of Jill's diaries, in which she wrote about her male friends at length. But, in mid-June 1999, police found a partial palm print on her front gate after forensic scientists had used state-of-the-art techniques to study it – and the front door – for clues, which was believed to have come from the killer. Police were hopeful that, as the print did not belong to anyone known to Jill, or to regular callers at the house including the postman, it would belong to the killer. The bullet used to murder the TV presenter also provided a vital clue in that it had a unique personal "trademark" – detectives discovered six tiny scratch marks etched into the brass cartridge case. It was believed that the killer either loaded his own rounds and squeezed or hit the case to ensure a snug fit, or that he may have reduced the charge in the cartridge to lessen the noise it made. Motives for the attack continued to elude police.

Meanwhile, Jon Roseman, Jill's agent, was quizzed by police after he came forward with an unpublished manuscript he had spent four years writing about a serial killer murdering TV stars. The book was finished prior to the presenter's death, but one plotline involved a victim being gunned down outside their own home. He was not considered a suspect by police.

In September 1999, the investigating team had been scaled down and the list of key suspects was reduced to 80 individuals. By this time, police had taken 1,000 witness statements and had interviewed 2,500 people. They had read more than 1,000 documents, 3,500 letters and messages sent to the incident room, and 13,700 emails sent direct to the BBC. They had watched footage from 191 security cameras and examined more than 1,000 items from the scene of the shooting. Although still confident they would catch the killer, they were still no nearer finding him or uncovering the motive for the attack.

In December, detectives found an automatic pistol in the River Thames near Putney Bridge, less than a mile from where Jill was murdered. Ballistic experts examined the gun, trying to match it to the bullet, but it was not the murder weapon. Then, in January 2000, it came to light that a mystery man had called Jill's utility providers claiming to be her brother and asking for her bills to be sent to him at her home address in November 1998. The man used the internet service 192.com to gain information on the presenter's home address although he was unable to get a telephone number for her. He was eventually traced but not arrested by police. A £5 million appeal was launched by Sophie, the Countess of Wessex, in Jill's memory in March 2000. By the following month, 20 new names were being checked by police following a fresh appeal on *Crimewatch*.

More than a year after the murder, a man named Barry Bulsara (previously known as Barry George) – who lived just 750 yards from Jill Dando's former home – was questioned by detectives after he was arrested on "suspicion of murder". Bulsara had offered information to police on the murder on the first anniversary of the victim's death and he was finally arrested after a month's surveillance. He appeared in court, charged with the murder on 29th May 2000, and was remanded in custody. At a subsequent court appearance at the Old Bailey on 26th February 2001, Bulsara came face to face with Jill's fiancé Alan Farthing for the first time as well as Nick Ross, the co-presenter of

*Crimewatch*. Bulsara denied murdering Jill Dando. He was represented by Michael Mansfield, a top defence lawyer.

Three witnesses had picked out Bulsara from an identity parade. He was described in court as being obsessed with celebrities and guns and as having followed the murder closely, acting in a strange manner. He told a friend at the time: "I was there, you know." Evidence against Bulsara was given, including a forensic discovery on a coat found at his home in Cookham Road, Fulham. An obsessed fan of rock legend Freddie Mercury (real name Farrokh Bulsara), Bulsara was accused of being capable of the crime because he held a grudge against the BBC for insulting the Queen star. His surname had, by this time, been changed legally to that of his idol. The court was told how the accused also had pictures of Anthea Turner and had used the name Steve Majors, after Lee Majors of *The Six Million Dollar Man* fame. He was described as living in a fantasy world of TV stars and even told one passenger on a bus that he was Freddie Mercury's cousin and that he was going to be late for Jill Dando's memorial service.

As S F Majors, he had served in the Territorial Army for nearly a year in 1981, where he had undertaken weapons courses, which involved firing, stripping and assembling self-loading rifles and machine guns. Bulsara, with his moustache and goatee beard, looked up to the gallery packed with spectators at his trial. While taking notes and sipping from a glass of water, he listened intently as the prosecution, led by Orlando Pownall, presented its case against him. The jury were warned by the judge, Mr Justice Gage, that the trial could last as long as eight weeks.

QC Michael Mansfield argued against the prosecution's case,

saying that for Jill to have been murdered by such precision with a single muffled shot (yet no silencer was used), the killer had to have been a professional assassin. Mansfield went on to tell the court that the case against the defendant was hanging by the merest of threads and "tore" at the police case with regard to Bulsara's coat, which had been removed from his home and which contained a single speck of firearms residue that matched three similar particles in Jill's hair. He added that it had only been examined by scientists after being kept in a police exhibits store and then photographed in a studio where firearms from previous unrelated cases had been pictured. He claimed that the residue was unlike a DNA trace or even a shoe mark and that it was one of five types commonly encountered by experts, and he went on to state that the coat had been contaminated while in police storage. He gave the jury 12 reasons why Bulsara did not kill the TV presenter, including the fact that he had no motive to do so. In summing up, the judge advised the jury to set aside emotion when deciding the fate of Barry Bulsara on 25th June 2001.

The defendant was, however, convicted of murder and jailed for life on 2nd July that same year. By 4th July 2001, he was on suicide watch in Belmarsh prison. He was granted leave of appeal by the end of the year, by which time he was serving his sentence at Whitemoor jail in Cambridgeshire. When the case came to appeal in July 2002, his QC, Michael Mansfield, hit out at the judge who jailed him, claiming there were no fingerprints, no footprints and no DNA evidence against the convicted man. However, the judges rejected the appeal on the grounds that identity evidence put Bulsara in the area at the right time, there was firearms residue discovered on his coat, a fibre found on Jill matched the killer's clothes, and he had been pictured holding a gun like the murder weapon. Additionally, he was obsessed with Jill and other celebrities, he made a flawed alibi statement to detectives, and he lied when interviewed by police. The Appeal judges said that the evidence was compelling and that the conviction was correct. Nevertheless, Barry's family, including his 66-year-old mother, Margaret, vowed to continue their case until he was found to be innocent.

New doubts over the forensic evidence against Bulsara came to light in 2007 and he was granted a second appeal against his conviction. Strathclyde police experts were brought in to re-examine the fibres and found they were not the same. It was suggested in newspaper reports – especially following a *Panorama* programme in September 2006 which highlighted the case – that if the interpretation of the evidence at the time had been different the original jury may have found the defendant not guilty. The Criminal Cases Review Commission also investigated Bulsara's conviction from 2004 onwards. Even Dr Robin Keeley, expert witness for the prosecution, had serious doubts over the case against Bulsara. He later said that the key piece of evidence, the residue from the firearm, was not significant and should have been treated as "neutral" in the case and not as "compelling evidence", as outlined by the prosecution. On 15th November 2007 it was decided that Bulsara would once again stand trial for the murder of Jill Dando when the Court of Appeal judges quashed his conviction after ruling it unsafe. The case was brought to appeal by the Criminal Cases Review Commission, which felt that too much weight had been put on the speck of firearms residue found in his pocket. It was a small victory for his family, but another trial would stir up memories for the victim's family more than eight years after she was shot.

Bulsara had been arrested more than a year after the presenter's death when police received a tip-off about him and his obsessive stalking behaviour, but the leads about him were buried in the avalanche of information flowing into police shortly after Jill's death. The retrial was under way by the middle of 2008 and he was found not guilty on 1st August that year. Bulsara, a loner with mental problems and a low IQ, was expected to demand compensation of around £1 million for the seven years he had spent in prison for the wrongful conviction of the murder of Jill Dando. It was thought that, with no new leads, police were unlikely to reopen the case but, in February 2009, new allegations that a Serbian hitman had murdered the TV presenter were being investigated after a petty criminal was alleged to have confessed in a crowded bar in Belgrade that he had committed the murder in revenge for the NATO bombing in 1999. As of early 2012, no new evidence has come to light and Jill Dando's family are no nearer to seeing justice for their loved one than they were on 26th April 1999.

# Multiple Deaths

## Brighton Trunk Murders

(1934)

On 17th June 1934, an unusual smell was noticed coming from an unclaimed plywood trunk as it lay in the left luggage office of Brighton station. The police were alerted by cloakroom attendant William Vinnicombe, and the torso of a woman was discovered inside the trunk once it was inspected. The victim's legs were discovered in a case left at King's Cross station in London but the woman's arms and head were never found. Dubbed "pretty feet" due to her beautiful dancer's feet, a post-mortem revealed that the young woman was around five months' pregnant and around 25 years old. In an amazing prediction to a daily newspaper, American clairvoyant Gene Dennis claimed that the young woman was killed on 3rd June 1934 and that she had long hair and wore glasses. She went on to state that the murderer was a small man with a dark moustache and short dark hair who was well dressed, not poor, and who wore a blue striped shirt open at the neck. Dennis also believed the murderer to have an impediment to his speech. She also predicted that while police were searching for the murderer of the young victim they would find another, totally unrelated murderer who was mentally deranged in some way. Dennis also gave the police information about a blue car, which was connected to the case, and had the letter X and the numbers nine and one in its registration plate.

Dennis was adamant that the murder was connected to another murder in some way which, if it were not for the body parts of the first victim, would never have been discovered. She also claimed that the murder had something to do with the cotton business and that the word Stafford was involved somehow; the clairvoyant went on later to state that Stafford was where she pictured the murderer buying the suitcases. Actually, a piece of paper with the word "FORD" had been found in Brighton and Dennis felt that the murderer had been somewhere close to water. She predicted that two murders would be linked by the string (the murderer had wrapped the parts of the body in paper and then tied these with string). She described it as small rope or binder string, which was unbleached.

Owing to clues already found, the police were searching for the head in the Newcastle area. Dennis did not know this but did predict that the police search would take them to the north of England. She claimed that the young victim had been killed out in the open and that she was connected to her killer by a seed store. Dennis went on to state that she knew the girl had been taken from a car and onto a hard surface near a railroad. She claimed that the body was cut up crudely by the attacker using a jagged-edged knife or implement at night close to a boat factory (the clairvoyant could see a yellow boat) and that the murderer was aged between 33 and 35 years of age. Speaking to a reporter, Gene Dennis assured the interviewer that the murderer would be found.

Meanwhile, the post-mortem revealed the victim's age; the police had previously thought the body to be that of a woman in her 40s or 50s. Carrying out the examination, Sir Bernard Spilsbury also confirmed that Dennis was right in her prediction about the time of the death (as it was no more than three weeks previous to 17th June). This was further confirmed when newspapers found that both suitcases had the date of 2nd June 1934 on them. The papers had come from the *Daily Mail*, which circulated within a 50-mile radius of London. Spilsbury also confirmed that the girl had been dismembered by a hacksaw. Internal organs were sent to London to be examined to see if the young woman had been poisoned.

The first major hurdle for the investigating officers was the lack of a head or arms for the victim. Without them, identifying the pregnant woman was nigh on impossible. The only clue available was a piece of brown paper in which the body had been wrapped. A fragment of paper had the letters "FORD" scrawled roughly in blue pencil but the letters above it – which may have formed part of another word – were obscured by a thick clot of blood that had seeped through the cotton wool (in which the body was wrapped first) and onto the brown paper. The fragment of paper was carefully photographed by police and sent, along with the string used to tie the torso, to the Home Office, where special tests were applied to the paper. Hopes at the time were high that experts would be able to remove the blood clot and discover the missing letters underneath it.

Police, however, believed that the murderer was not local to

Brighton and, as no women were listed as missing in the area, they suspected that the murderer had deliberately dumped the body at the seaside resort in order to mislead any investigation into who the victim was and where she had come from. Women's clothing was found in Wimbledon, London, in a case, but it wasn't bloodstained; however, police did investigate the discovery in case the items belonged to their unidentified victim.

As police investigated further, more intriguing facts came to light. By the end of June 1934, a photograph of the paper fragment was seen by a shopkeeper in Sheffield who – having seen the writing on the brown paper – immediately called to speak to her next-door neighbour Phoebe Ford, who confirmed the "FORD" as being her signature. She also told police about her concerns for her 23-year-old married daughter, Phoebe Morley. Mrs Ford described to police how she had written her own name in the paper lining of the lid in the corner of a trunk similar to the one recovered in Brighton. She had written her name using a small "f", which was her usual way of signing her name. She explained that beneath the green paper lining of the trunk was a layer of brown paper, and she thought that the writing had penetrated through the layers from green to brown. Her claims were backed up by her husband. However, the Fords' daughter, having let her parents take her three-year-old daughter Mavis back to Sheffield with them some time before, turned up unharmed at a hostel in Folkestone where she had been taken in when she found herself homeless. She claimed she had given the paper to a German woman in Folkestone.

More than a dozen lines of inquiry were followed up by police but they still didn't know who the victim was, where she had been murdered or the identity of her killer. However, a vital clue became a real possibility for police on 22nd June 1934 when two knives, believed to have dismembered the victim, came into their possession. The knives were sent from Brighton to Scotland Yard, where Dr Roche Lynch carried out tests on them to ascertain whether they had in fact been used in the crime. The knives were tested to see if they had bloodstains belonging to the same blood group as the victim. In addition, he tested to see if any other blood was found within the trunk, in case the murderer had cut himself and his blood could also be found. Newspaper reports were critical of how the case was handled. Many thought that there should be a leading investigating officer, rather than local Brighton police and Scotland Yard grudgingly working side by side. Scotland Yard senior officers, with their undoubted great experience, had no control over what the local police were doing, or how they were doing it, and complaints that they were following differing lines of inquiry were rife. Also, delays in making vital announcements, including the fact that the victim had been pregnant, happened. After a number of reports about the inquiries being held up by a conflict of views between police forces, a statement was released by the investigating team to let the public know that they were working in harmony. The statement also read that there had been no developments in the case and that the police were no nearer a solution.

On 25th June 1934, an anonymous man signing himself "Londoner" sent a letter to Chief Inspector Donaldson at the Brighton police headquarters. The police immediately launched an appeal for the man to come forward. Details of the letter were kept a closely guarded secret, but it was clear that it did contain at least circumstantial evidence about the murder, including facts that had not been made public. Two days later the police announced that a man was under suspicion for the murder of the young woman, although no immediate arrest was likely because there was not sufficient evidence of guilt. The county of Sussex was being combed meticulously for missing evidence, while part of the investigation took police to Colchester and Chelmsford. By this point, it was believed that police knew where the brown paper that the torso had been wrapped in had come from. Detectives visited a shop in north London and uncovered certain information, but it was envisaged that police inquiries would take some time as it was understood that new developments, related to the change in ownership of cars and visits to a seaside resort on the east coast by two male friends, had occurred. By the end of June, police were convinced that the dismembering of the body had taken place in Sussex, although they had gathered vital evidence from various places in London including King's Cross (where the suitcase containing the victim's legs and feet were found) and Kentish Town.

In early July, police established where the trunk containing the torso had come from. The suitcase had already been identified by its makers the previous week. In addition, police were speculating that the murdered victim was possibly a convicted woman whose fingerprints had already been taken by colleagues. What was still baffling police, however, was why the woman's hands and arms had not been disposed of in the same way as her torso, legs and feet. In a bid to try and discover more clues, a description of the suitcase containing the woman's legs and feet was circulated. Made by Messrs B Lewis & Co of Church Road, Leyton, with locks and handles by Cheney & Son of Birmingham, the suitcase measured 26 inches by 15 inches by eight inches, and had two nickel-plated locks. It was the third principal clue, after the brown paper and the cabin trunk, released to the public. But, the case remained a mystery. In an unusual move, police then began issuing the names of 1,000 missing girls in a process of elimination which they hoped would lead to the identification of their victim. The first 10 names were released to the newspapers on 7th July 1934 and included Mabel Barton (21) from Ashford in Kent, Joan Thomas (20) from Tunbridge Wells, Kathleen Smith (25) from Worthing and Dorothy Kirk (24) from Dover. Other names were Ellen Warren (18) from Croydon, Mary Pugh (28) from Walmer in Kent, Florence Goldsack (24) from Dover, Amy Fairhurst (23) from Haywards Heath, Phyllis Fifer (24) from Portslade and Beryl Fooks (20) from Lancing in Sussex. Without a positive identification of their victim, police were simply unable to piece all the other evidence together.

The police had by this time changed their minds and were confident that their victim was murdered locally, either close to Brighton or Hove, and that she was local. They were so desperate to identify their victim that an appeal for information was also extended to the continent and police in various European countries were encouraged to co-operate with the investigation. In July, another list of women was circulated via the press while the disappearance of a young woman from Jersey – who had travelled to England but had suddenly stopped writing letters home and ceased to answer any letters she was sent from the island – was being seriously looked into.

A breakthrough came later that month when a tip-off from someone based near Portsmouth led police to a house in Patcham – three miles outside Brighton – where an extensive search of the gardens for the victim's missing head began. It ultimately led to nothing and, seven hours later, the search was called off by Chief Inspector Donaldson despite the information coming from reliable sources. The disappearance of the missing girl from Jersey, 24-year-old Larienne Lousse, was still under investigation at this time and police knew she had left her island home in the company of a man who claimed to come from Richmond; after arriving in Weston-super-Mare, the young woman's letters stopped at the end of May. Another lead was a man seen at Dartford station with a trunk, who changed trains at London Bridge bound for Brighton on the day that the torso was discovered. Via the newspapers, the man was assured of anonymity by police if he agreed to come forward to explain his movements on the day in question. The man in question eventually did come forward and was found to be unconnected to the case.

When 26-year-old Toni Mancini took lodgings at 52 Kemp Street in Brighton, close to the railway station, in 1933, he little realized that the murder he had committed in May 1934 would be discovered by police. However, during their investigations into the trunk murder, police carried out house-to-house enquiries and stumbled upon a trunk at the end of Mancini's bed in which the body of Violet Kaye was hidden. Visitors to the house had complained on several occasions of the smell at the premises but until the police arrived in an unconnected matter, Mancini (real name Cecil Lois England), thought he had got away with the murder of the 42-year-old. Petty criminal Mancini (also known as Jack Notyre, Tony English, Tony England and Antoni Pirillie) had a criminal record for loitering and theft. He had moved to Brighton in September 1933 with Kaye (real name Saunders; Violet Kaye was her stage name), a dancer and prostitute, from London where he worked as a waiter and bouncer. The couple were prone to arguments and had a particularly heated altercation in May 1934 at a café on Brighton's seafront where Mancini was working. The London dancer was never seen again and was believed by family and friends to have left the country for Paris. He gave some of her clothes and belongings to a teenage waitress called Elizabeth Attrell, with whom Saunders had accused him of having a relationship. Mrs Saunders' sister received a telegram from her to advise her that she had taken a job abroad; however, police discovered after finding the body that, by the time the message was received, the victim was already dead.

After being questioned by police when Saunders disappeared, Mancini went on the run but was eventually found in south London, where he was arrested. He was brought back to Brighton Police Court on 18th July 1934 and holidaymakers flocked to see the "trunk" murderer.

The case of the torso in the trunk was investigated in parallel with the death of Saunders, whom, it was established, was dead before the trunk at the station in Brighton was discovered. But there were marked differences in the two cases. Whoever had murdered and disposed of the first trunk had gone to great lengths to conceal the victim's identity. Mancini had made no effort to do the same. The first body was mutilated, but Mrs Saunders had been found intact. The police were anxious to point out that the two cases seemed entirely unrelated apart from the fact that both bodies were found in trunks, but they were mindful that the possibility of it being a separate and distinctly different crime seemed too much of a coincidence to be credible. Mancini had killed Saunders with a blow to the back of the head at their previous premises, before he wheeled her body in the trunk to Kemp Street where he shared a room with Bernard Schakter. Mancini's room-mate described the murderer as unable to sleep, prone to staring at the ceiling like a madman and desperate for a way to make it to America. Mancini, on one occasion, also threatened to cut up anyone who annoyed him and even took out a dagger from his drawer in the bedroom the two men shared. The room was small and Schakter had asked Mancini to remove the trunk from the room. The murderer had agreed to this but, in the weeks they shared the room, never did anything about it.

Meanwhile, police continued to receive and gather information about the first trunk case and were led to a shop on the sea front, where similar sash-cord to that with which the torso was tied and cotton wool with oil stains was removed from the premises. Police had a man they believed was connected to the case under 24-hour surveillance. The suspect had already been questioned by police and they were sure that he held vital information about the facts relating to the murder. By the end of July 1934, developments had led police to dig up the brick floor at an unoccupied flat in Park Crescent, Brighton, at 2.00am; to have a meeting with the Director of Public Prosecutions with regard to a possible charge of murder; and to trace an important witness in London. The flat had, at one time, been occupied by Violet Saunders, and the name Violet Kaye was clearly displayed on the electric meter. In August 1934, police announced that they wished to interview a naval man who needed to be traced in Brighton in connection with the first trunk crime.

When Mancini came to trial on 10th August, he stated that he had found Violet Kaye dead on the bed and that he had been too afraid to tell anyone as he had no way of proving he didn't murder the 42-year-old woman. He talked of a man called Kay Fredericks with whom the deceased had had a five-year relationship. He claimed that Fredericks, from Chelsea in London, wanted Violet Saunders back, but she wouldn't go. Mancini claimed that all he was guilty of was keeping the body once he had found the victim dead. The hammer head used to kill Violet Saunders had been found at the house in Park Crescent. It was presented to the court by G A Paling, the prosecutor, while a 17-year-old girl, Doris Saville, gave dramatic evidence when she relayed how she and a friend had met two men in a park in London. One of the men, identified as Mancini, had spoken to the girl of a murder and told her he was innocent. He had asked the girl to give him a false alibi and she had agreed. Witnesses also gave evidence to say that Mancini and Saunders had appeared to be a contented couple, and the quality and nature of the forensic evidence was brought into question. As a result, in just over two hours, the court returned a verdict of not guilty.

Mancini allegedly confessed in 1976 what really happened on the day Saunders died. He told a reporter how she had attacked him with the hammer during a huge row and that he had wrestled her for it. After he had managed to take the hammer from the victim she had demanded it back. When he threw it, the hammer hit Saunders on the left temple and she died. He claimed he hadn't told the truth before as he believed he would not have had a fair trial.

Almost a year after the first trunk case, police were still making inquiries, which led them to robberies committed in the north London area. It was believed that a man who lived in the neighbourhood around the time of the first murder would be able to help with their inquiries. However, no new leads ever provided any real evidence for the police to work with: the identity of the dismembered victim is still a mystery and her unknown assailant was not brought to justice. Gene Dennis's predictions, which came true in part, were never fully realized.

# Jack the Stripper and the Hammersmith Murders

(1959–1965)

Elizabeth Figg, from Upper Holloway, London, was found strangled on 17th June 1959. The 21-year-old's body was discovered on a towpath near the Thames at Chiswick at 5.00am. For 48 hours, her identity was a mystery until an artist's drawing was circulated in the press and a friend, Pauline Mills, came forward to put a name to the attractive face. Pauline told police that Elizabeth had friends on Bayswater Road close to Hyde Park, who might have seen a man in a car pick her up there on Tuesday 16th June. Police believed that Elizabeth had been strangled and then taken to the riverside where her body was propped in a "natural" position against a willow tree. One theory being investigated was that she had accepted a lift from a man who had then strangled her with his bare hands.

Elizabeth, known to her landlord as "Ann", had been living in her lodgings for just two weeks, after answering a postcard in a shop window about a room for rent. He confirmed that "Ann" had left home between 6.00pm and 7.00pm on the Tuesday evening wearing a pretty black-and-white dress. Elizabeth had told her landlord that she worked in a café in the West End. He confirmed Pauline's story that the victim was quiet and usually stayed at home in the evenings. She hadn't told her landlord where she had come from and he didn't ask his new tenant. In fact, Elizabeth had moved to London from her home city of Liverpool just 18 months before she was killed. Was she the first victim of a serial killer who became notorious as Jack the Stripper?

Named after serial killer Jack the Ripper, who operated in London's Whitechapel area in 1888, Jack the Stripper strangled prostitutes and left them naked in and around Hammersmith between 1964 and 1965. Although Elizabeth's death happened somewhat earlier than this and didn't fit the pattern the murderer came to be familiar for, police did believe that she could have been his first victim. The Stripper eventually had six known murders attributed to him, but two other women could also have been his victims. This has never been proved or disproved and Jack the Stripper was never caught.

Police know that the young woman from Liverpool was seen at around 1.10am on the morning she died, near Holland Park underground station, and that less than four hours later she was dead. On Tuesday 16th June, Elizabeth was seen talking to a number of men in different cars wearing her black-and-white striped dress. She was known to solicit men in their vehicles rather than take them to her room. She was dropped at just after 1.00am at Holland Park station by Ernest Forrest, a builder and decorator who had picked Elizabeth up at around 11.30pm. Forrest told a court hearing in August 1959 that he had wanted to spend the night with the young woman but she said she had plans to meet someone at the tube station. They had then arranged to meet at 3.30am. Forrest waited for Elizabeth to return, but she did not arrive, and he was surprised when two police officers turned up to find out why he was parked without his car lights on. Detective Superintendent James Mitchell told the court hearing that there was no trace of the woman's movements after 1.10am, while Home Office pathologist Dr Teare estimated that by 2.00am Elizabeth Figg was dead.

Four years later, in September 1963, the naked, headless body of a girl was found in a rubbish dump just a few feet away from the Thames towpath at Mortlake, between the Chiswick and Kew bridges. A mechanical shovel lifting loads of ash to be used in roadworks unearthed the body from a pit and the driver of the shovel saw legs dangling from the front of his vehicle. It was believed that the victim had lain underneath two feet of tightly packed ash at the dump – owned by Barnes council – for several months. The girl was named in November 1963 as 22-year-old Gwynneth Rees, who had moved to London from Barry in South Wales in 1958. Like Elizabeth Figg, the victim had been strangled. Also like Elizabeth she was known by other names including Georgette Rees, Tina Smart and Tina Dawson. She had previously lived in Stepney in the East End, but had moved to Battersea in August 1963. Was Gwynneth Jack the Stripper's second victim?

Another victim who also had a number of aliases was 31-year-old Hannah Tailford, who moved to London from Northumberland in 1959. She was found naked in the Thames close to where the first two victims had been discovered. The good-time girl had two children – three-year-old Linda and an 18-month-old son – who police were desperately trying to find when their mother's body was discovered in February 1964. By April that same year, there was a fourth victim, who was found naked just a mile from where Hannah's body was recovered. The woman, who was said to be aged between 25 and 30 years old, was found near Duke's Meadow, Chiswick, on the Thames towpath. She had drowned, but across her chest was a wound around an inch long. The naked body of the fifth victim was also found in the Thames, near Chiswick, in early November 1964, and was identified as 29-year-old Irene Lockwood – she was the third prostitute to be found dead in the Chiswick area that year. The victim was a close friend of another prostitute, 22-year-old Vicki Pender, who was found strangled in a flat in Finsbury Park (although Vicki's killer had by then been convicted of her murder). Vicki had, however, lured wealthy men to nude parties where photographs were taken without the partygoers' knowledge. She had been beaten up on several occasions for trying to blackmail men shown with her in the photographs. Police believed that Irene, who had been working the same racket, had also been the victim of a man being blackmailed.

The sixth victim was former striptease artist Helene Barthelemy, aged 22, who was found strangled in a lovers' walk at Brentford. She was the fourth victim discovered within six months and, at the end of April 1964, Scotland Yard detectives began a hunt for a sex-crazed killer. Helene had entertained a mystery visitor at her flat in Talbot Road, Willesden, on Monday 20th April. She was last seen by a friend, Ivy Williams, at around 10.00pm that evening. Neighbours were worried when it was discovered that the young woman had not finished the washing up from the evening meal she and her visitor had shared and had left her flat door open. When her body was found at Brentford, police were able to establish that she had been murdered between midnight and 7.00am on 24th April, and that her body had been dumped in an alley off Swyncombe Avenue from a car or van. Detectives were convinced early on that the murder was almost certainly linked with the death of the last three victims (if not the first two as well) as clear marks of violence had been used against the women. Detectives believed that the man they were looking for was picking up girls in his vehicle and then taking them to isolated spots alongside the Thames, where he then indulged in a variety of perversions.

While police thought that Gwynneth Rees was suffocated before her body was dumped, they were convinced that both Hannah Tailford and Irene Lockwood were forced into the Thames by the killer and then held under until they drowned. As Helene was found in an alley, it was believed that the killer had been interrupted before he could dump her body in the river. Helene had worked as a striptease artist for three seasons on Blackpool's promenade, known as the "Golden Mile". Police thought this might give the case a connection to the earlier murders but, by 27th April 1964, they hit a "brick wall of silence" when, despite questioning 30 men, they were no further on in the murder investigation. By this time, four of the victims discovered in 1964 were thought to have belonged to a vice ring; it was believed that the men involved were keeping quiet due to fear of reprisals from vice-ring bosses. Helene had certainly been punished by her bosses; just a few days before she died she had had two teeth knocked out.

Gwynneth Rees had also been given a ferocious beating in the days before she died.

The four most recent victims all had their fingerprints on file with police and were known for working the Paddington, Notting Hill, Bayswater and Soho areas of London as prostitutes. It was known that the vice ring ran a booking service where girls were sent out to customers. Police decided to have a major crackdown on London vice rings and launched a huge investigation into the underworld, interviewing more than 120 known prostitutes. They were given a number of leads in their inquiries into the deaths of Gwynneth, Irene, Helene and Hannah, including the names and addresses of several men who made demands of vice girls. Four murder squads were working on the cases at London's Shepherd's Bush police station. Less than two months later, another body was found half-naked in the River Ouse in Buckingham.

One man was acquitted of one of the murders, dubbed the "River Nudes", when it was found he made a false confession. Kenneth Archibald (54) had told police that he was the man who strangled Irene Lockwood, but when he appeared on a murder charge at the Old Bailey on 23rd June he told the jury he had made it up. He was found not guilty and discharged. However, more witnesses were starting to come forward, especially those who had felt too frightened and intimidated to do so before. Many of them involved in London vice rings had feared the vengeance of their bosses, but the police were slowly beginning to persuade people to speak about their associations with the dead women.

However, the police were no closer to finding the killer by the time the next victim was found in July 1964. The nude woman, who had also been strangled, was 31-year-old Glasgow-born prostitute Mary Fleming. She was found in a quiet Chiswick cul-de-sac, in exactly the same way as Helene Barthelemy had been found and just three miles away from where the 22-year-old was discovered. Mary had been living in Notting Hill with her children, Veronica (2) and eight-month-old David. Like some of the other women, she also used an alternative name.

Despite the fact that Mary's death was linked to that of the others, the nude murders remained a mystery. By November 1964, police had interviewed thousands of people. They were then faced with their next victim, 23-year-old Margaret McGowan, who used the aliases Frances Brown, Frances Quinn, Anne Sutherland and Susan Edwards. Like the other victims, Margaret was a known prostitute and was found naked and dumped in west London. She had been strangled and her body hidden under rubble and a dustbin lid in a Civil Defence car park in Hornton Street, Kensington. Like Irene, she had been involved in a photo-blackmail racket (alongside Vicki Pender). Her case was added to the earlier crimes.

By the end of November, it was feared that Margaret's friend, June O'Neill, might have also been murdered. June had disappeared seven weeks earlier – about the time that Margaret was last seen alive – and police knew that she and Margaret had a number of men friends in common. Meanwhile, the whereabouts of Margaret's five-month-old son also remained a mystery. Her three-year-old daughter was living with Margaret's mother in Scotland, while her two-year-old son had been adopted by another family.

Margaret's lover, Paul Quinn, stated that she had laughed at the thought she might be murdered by a customer. Twenty-eight-year-old Quinn went on his own crusade to find his murdered girlfriend's killer, touring west London's pubs and clubs and talking to prostitutes who had known her. Quinn knew Margaret as Frances Brown – her real name – and found one of her best friends, a prostitute originally from South Wales, who was frightened by the killings.

She confirmed that many of the women working in London would now only see men that they knew and were fairly sure that they were safe with. She told Quinn that prostitutes were, more than ever, taking care of each other and if any woman left in a car with a man, another woman would write down the registration number. She also told him that she would do anything she could to help. Police believed that Margaret could have been suffocated as she slept at the killer's house. No marks of violence were found on her body (or the bodies of the earlier victims) and it was not established at the end of 1964 whether the killer had actually had sexual relations with any of the victims. The police believed he could have been impotent, or that he had an insane hatred of women. June O'Neill was eventually found safe and well in another part of London and confirmed that she had seen Margaret just days before her death. However, another witness, known as Miss X, had her identity kept secret as police were confident she was the last person known to have seen Margaret alive and her knowledge was invaluable to them.

In December 1964, police issued E-fit pictures of two men in a bid to help them find the killer of the five women murdered during the year. Miss X told police that she last saw Margaret (or Frances as she knew her) in October at the Warwick Castle pub in Notting Hill, where they each agreed to go with two men, who had cars nearby. Margaret got into a darkish-grey Ford Zephyr or Zodiac with a man who looked around 30 to 35 years old. Miss X described him as about five foot eight inches, with a stocky build and brown hair. He had a London accent and wore a light tan suede driving jacket with a sheepskin collar and a white shirt. If the two women separated during an evening, the usual plan was that they would meet up again outside the Jazz Club in Notting Hill. On 23rd October, Miss X turned up as arranged, but Margaret did not. Police appealed for the two men to come forward so they could be eliminated from their inquiries.

On 16th February 1965, a new hunt was under way when the naked body of a young woman in her 20s was found hidden under bracken behind a factory in west London. Yard detectives discovered the dead girl's identity later that day after tracing her back to a Hammersmith boarding house. Bridie Moor, or Bridie O'Hara as she was also known, was believed to have come from Ireland. Like a number of the other victims, Bridie was tattooed, and police immediately linked her murder to the five women killed the previous year. It was thought that Bridie, who had been strangled, may have lain undiscovered for several weeks before she was found. Probing yet again into London's vice world, detectives found a witness who saw 28-year-old Bridie on 11th January with a man in Hammersmith, the last day she was seen alive.

It was a vital clue in a case that was helped by a second clue, which gave detectives a fairly strong lead on where Bridie had been hidden before her body was dumped.

In the middle of February, it was reported in the papers that police were confident that the killer would soon be caught after they visited a house in the west London area. A number of items of women's clothing were removed from the house and it was divulged to the public that it was believed the killer was building a "Black Museum" of the clothes of his victims along with handbags and high-heeled shoes. Police also believed that the killer kept the bodies of his victims for up to three weeks before dumping them. Traces of dust found on Bridie O'Hara showed detectives the type of building that the killer used.

After the discovery of Bridie the killings stopped. One prime suspect, Mungo Ireland – a married man in his 40s – eventually committed suicide, but there was strong evidence to suggest that he had been in Scotland when the final victim was killed. Of the two other suspects, one was a real possibility. Harold Jones was convicted in 1921 at the age of 15 of murdering two young girls in his hometown of Abertillery, Wales. Due to his age he was not hanged and, after 20 years in jail, he was released at the age of 35 for exemplary behaviour. He moved to west London in 1947 where he married and had a daughter. Despite the fact that he was never considered as a suspect by police due to the lack of earlier records, his early murders were not dissimilar to the murders of at least six, if not eight, London women in this case whose killer has never been brought to justice. Here's what the police actually knew.

All the women were prostitutes in and around west London. They were all about five feet two inches tall. Three of them had tattoos. Two were probably drowned in a bath, or the Thames. Four were suffocated. Spots of paint were found on a number of the victims. All were stripped naked and even their jewellery was removed. None of their clothing or jewellery has ever been found. All appear to have been kept somewhere for a period after they were killed.

The police worked day and night to solve these crimes – the lights burned in the first floor window of the murder squad's investigation room for more than a year. They never discovered any significant clues that might lead them to the killer, and the person, or persons, responsible have never been punished for their crimes.

# The Lake Bodom Murders

(1960)

The beautiful surroundings of Lake Bodom – a three-kilometre by one-kilometre stretch of water close to the city of Espoo, the second largest city in Finland – was the backdrop to the murder of three teenagers (two girls and one boy) on 5th June 1960. The teenagers had been camping on the shores of the lake, some 22 kilometres west of Helsinki, with their friend Nils Wilhelm Gustafsson. At some point between 4.00am and 6.00am they were involved in a random attack which left three of them dead and Gustafsson, as the sole survivor, severely injured and in shock. The three victims were 15-year-old Ania Tuulikki Maki, 15-year-old Maila Irmeli Bjorklund and Seppo Antero Boisman who was 18 years old when he was killed. All three had been stabbed and bludgeoned. Eighteen-year-old Gustafsson was concussed and had fractures to his jaw and other bones in his face. The case remains unsolved and, as one of Finland's leading mysteries, sees new theories and possibilities about the murders introduced regularly. Police were baffled at who had carried out the attack and why the four teenagers were attacked as they lay sleeping in their tent.

The four youngsters had enjoyed a fun afternoon and evening on the shores of the lake in peaceful surroundings. They set up their tent and had no reason to suspect that they were about to become the victims of a gruesome attack.

The tent was not a big one, it was about one and a half metres wide, and the teenagers retired inside at around 10.30pm. The tent had come from Seppo Boisman's workplace and he had also managed to acquire some spirits and citrus liqueur. The boys were also carrying condoms – just in case they got lucky – which they had bought on the black market. The tent was set up in a camp in the grounds of the Oittaa Manor House on the edge of the city; it was pitched by the lake close to some large birch trees against which the boys rested their motorbikes. The lake was popular with night fishermen, but it wasn't clear whether the youngsters did any fishing that night. After going into the tent, the two girls slept to the sides of the tent while the two boys placed themselves in the middle.

It was daylight by the time the bodies of the three murdered teenagers were discovered. The collapsed tent was visible to some local youths who were birdwatching very early that morning – around 6.00am – although they admitted to police they were more interested in the motorcycles by the trees. They could clearly also see a person lying on top of the canvas, but they assumed that the individual they could see was either still asleep or sunbathing. What they didn't realize was that it was an extremely badly injured Gustafsson. The youths also saw a blonde-haired man walking away at the back of the tent. The man was never traced during the ensuing investigation, although he was also spotted by a lone teenage boy who was fishing on an islet not far from the murder scene.

Police finally arrived on the scene at around midday when a local carpenter happened to walk past the tent at around 11.00am that morning. The victims had been attacked from outside the tent and the canvas was slashed. Gustafsson was found on top of the tent by the passer-by. When police were called to the scene they were met with a chilling sight as three young adults lay brutally slain before them underneath the collapsed brown tent. The tent and pieces of clothing, along with other evidence, were kept by police in the hope that advances in testing would become available and the killer would at last be caught.

Gossip about the murders was rife around the local area and some believed that they knew the identity of the murderer. Some locals were convinced that he was Valdemar Gyllström, a local kiosk-owner, who incidentally confessed to the killings four times before his own death. He had threatened his wife into giving him an alibi at the time of the murders, but she later admitted that he had not been at home with her on the night of the murders. Gyllström eventually drowned himself in the lake in 1969. In addition, however, several others were also suspected of the tragic crime including a German man, Hans Assmann, who even confessed to the murders on his deathbed. But no proof was ever found that he was responsible and the police confirmed that he had in fact had an alibi for the morning of the attack.

No killer was ever found or brought to justice but, in 2004, police believed that after 44 years they had enough evidence to convict the fourth teenager and sole survivor of the incident – Gustafsson. The Finnish National Bureau of Investigation claimed that the case could be solved and Gustafsson's guilt proved by new analysis of the bloodstains found at the scene because his dead girlfriend – with whom he had been having a relationship for just three weeks prior to her death – had received the most injuries. The 15-year-old girl was stabbed multiple times.

The Finnish court heard how the then 18-year-old had been so badly injured that it would have been impossible for him to have killed his friends. However, the prosecution argued that DNA profiling cast suspicion on Gustafsson and called for life imprisonment. He was acquitted of the crime in 2005 at the age of 64, having spent considerable time on remand for a crime that the authorities just didn't believe he had committed.

# Bible John

(1968–1969)

Convicted of double rape in 1993, violent and sadistic Peter Tobin spent 10 years in prison for sexual attacks on two young girls, whom he had held at knifepoint, forcing them to drink strong alcohol, before turning on the gas and leaving them for dead. The victims survived and Tobin, who then went on the run, was caught hiding out within a religious sect in the West Midlands. His life up to this point had been one littered with crime and violence against women. The youngest of seven children, Tobin had been sent to an approved school at the tender age of seven because he was an extremely difficult child who obviously had major problems outside the scope of his family.

Tobin was released from jail in 2004 after serving his time for the double rape but, just three years later, was sentenced to life – with the recommendation to serve a minimum of 21 years – for the rape and murder of Angelika Kluk, which he committed in 2006 in Glasgow, Scotland. He was subsequently found guilty of the murders of two more women who went missing in 1991 when their remains were found at his former home in Margate, Kent. His minimum sentence was extended to 30 years. There has been much speculation that Tobin is also the serial killer "Bible John" who killed three women in the Glasgow area in the late 1960s. But is he?

Patricia Docker's body was found on 23rd February 1968. The 25-year-old had been strangled, but the police investigation was hampered when it was discovered, two months after Patricia's death, that she'd been at the Barrowland Ballroom and not the Majestic Ballroom as she had told her parents the night before she died. In August 1969, there were rumours that children playing in an old building in MacKeith Street had seen the body of a woman. The rumours were dismissed as a wild fantasy on the part of the children, but 32-year-old Jemima McDonald was missing after a night out at Barrowland Ballroom and her sister was concerned enough to go and see for herself. What she found was the battered body of the mother of three, who had been raped, strangled and beaten to death. When the police began their investigation, it was discovered that Jemima had been seen leaving the dance hall around midnight with a tall, slim man with reddish hair. A third victim also visited the Barrowland Ballroom that year.

On 30th October, 29-year-old Helen Puttock had been to the club with her sister Jean. The two women met a couple of men at the club, both called John. After spending more than an hour together, the foursome left the club and one of the men headed for a bus in George Square. Helen, Jean and the second man named John got in a taxi together. In the Scotstoun area, Jean got out of the taxi believing that it was bound for Helen's home in Earl Street and that her sister was safe. The following morning, Helen's body was found in the back garden of her flat. Like Patricia, Helen had been raped and strangled. Her handbag had been rifled through and the contents strewn nearby but the actual bag was missing. Helen's body was battered and there was a deep bite mark on her leg.

By this time, although there was no concrete evidence that the killer was the same man that had murdered Patricia and Jemima, the police thought it highly likely. The man that Jean met said his name was John "Templeton" or "Sempleson" and repeatedly quoted from the Bible. She described him as tall and slim with reddish to fair hair. Jean stated to police that the man was well dressed, young, extremely polite and well spoken. He had told Jean the night before that he believed dance halls were dens of iniquity. However, other witnesses – including the bouncers at the club – described the man that Jean was talking about as short with black hair, although a further witness had also heard him describe Barrowland as a "den of iniquity". Jean was incredibly drunk the night she left the club with Helen and the man calling himself John so it is possible that her description was inaccurate. At around 1.30am on the night Helen was killed, a young, smartly dressed man fitting the description of Bible John was seen heading towards the north side of the River Clyde ferry.

Police were determined to catch Bible John, but they had very little to go on. The first victim, Patricia, hadn't been where they thought she was, so witnesses were unable to give much information by the time that the police tracked them down. Jemima's night out at Barrowland Ballroom didn't throw up any significant clues and Jean's description of the killer was possibly unreliable. Despite this, a number of suspects were questioned but no arrests were made. Interestingly, all three victims had been menstruating at the time they were murdered, and tampons and other sanitary products were placed on or near the three women. Each woman's handbag was also missing – which led the police to believe that the killer had taken them as a trophy – and all three had been strangled with their own stockings.

Years after the murders, police exhumed the body of former Scots Guard John Irvine McInnes from his grave in Lanarkshire in order to test for DNA matches against semen found on Helen's tights. The tests, carried out in 1996, proved inconclusive. However, there were striking similarities between the murders in Glasgow in 1968 and 1969 and that of Angelika Kluk, a Polish student on a working holiday in Glasgow at the time of her death. She was last seen in the company of Tobin who, calling himself "Pat McLaughlin", was working at St Patrick's Roman Catholic Church as a handyman. He was using a different name at this time in order to avoid detection by police and the probation service, given that he was still a registered sex offender following his conviction for the double rape in 1994. Police knew that Tobin's three former wives had been subjected to violent treatment at his hands. All three were raped by him and severely beaten as well as being imprisoned. Tobin had also throttled all three on more than one occasion. In addition, there are striking similarities between Tobin's appearance and that of an artist's impression of Bible John in the 1960s.

Tobin had been living in Glasgow at the end of the 1960s and had moved from there in 1969 following his first marriage. He met his first wife at Barrowland Ballroom in 1969 and it is known that Tobin was driven to violence by a woman's menstrual cycle. This had long been suspected by police as being the motive behind the Bible John killings.

Helen's sister, Jean McLachlan, died in 2010 at the age of 74;

she was the only known woman to have seen Bible John close up, and although DNA might be a possibility in order to prove Tobin guilty of the three murders, police believe that poor storage of any samples will make this virtually impossible. There are those that do not believe all three women were murdered by Bible John. Some believe that the first murder, of Patricia Docker, could have been carried out by a different man. But, the evidence suggests that in all likelihood these three cruel murders were perpetrated by one killer and many believe that the man responsible is Peter Tobin.

# The Monster of Florence

(1968–1985)

In August 1968, six-year-old Natalino Mele was asleep on the back seat of the car in which his mother, 32-year-old Barbara Locci, and her lover, 29-year-old Antonio Lo Bianco, were enjoying a sexual liaison, when they were brutally shot dead by an unknown assailant. The child was either taken from the car by the killer and left on the doorstep of a nearby house at 2.00am in the morning or, on finding his mother and his "uncle" dead, he fled on his own to the door, on which he knocked in the early hours. He was so traumatized that even he didn't know how he got there.

Barbara Locci (nicknamed "Queen Bee" for her many extramarital relationships) was married to Natalino's father, Stefano Mele, and lived in Lastra a Signa in the province of Florence, Italy, with her family. Her murder, along with that of her lover Bianco, was the first of 16 murders of couples in cars, which would stretch across almost two decades of cold-blooded killings. Bianco and Locci were returning home from the cinema on 21st August when they noticed that the young child lay asleep in the back of the car. Knowing they had time for a sexual encounter before they made it home, Barbara's lover began removing her clothes once they parked in a local cemetery. Before they had got very far, a lone figure appeared out of the darkness and shot them both dead with a .22 Beretta.

When Natalino Mele knocked on the door of the farmhouse tears were pouring down his face, and he told the farmer that his mother and "uncle" – the term he used for all his mother's lovers – were dead. When police were called to the scene, they discovered eight shell casings by the vehicle, but were baffled as to who the perpetrator was or why the crime had been committed. They arrived at Natalino's family home to question his father at around 7.00am the following morning, after the initial investigation had begun. Stefano Mele agreed to accompany the detectives to the police station, where he gave them the names of a number of men known to be his late wife's lovers. He did not seem particularly surprised by the news and, having been questioned at length, was asked to return to the police station the following day. He had suggested to police that any one of his wife's lovers could have committed the crime but, on 23rd August 1968, he walked back into the police station and confessed to the killings himself. He gave a detailed description of how he and a friend, Salvatore Vinci, had seen the couple leaving the cinema and had followed them to the graveyard. He described how he was fed up with his wife's infidelities and the fact that she so openly humiliated him in front of friends and neighbours. Mele claimed that Vinci handed him a weapon and he simply killed the couple as they made out in Antonio Lo Bianco's Alfa Romeo. However, he failed to mention his son or what had happened to him.

Mele was quickly arrested and the following day police began hunting for the gun in the area where he said he had disposed of it, but to no avail. The arrested father then changed his story and claimed he had given the gun back to his accomplice, Vinci. He then went on to retract his confession and began blaming Salvatore's brother, Francesco Vinci, instead. For a number of days, Mele kept changing his story but, two years after his wife's and her lover's death, he was found guilty of their murders and was sentenced to 14 years in prison on the grounds of insanity.

By the time eight years had passed since the murders of Barbara and Antonio, Mele had spent six of those years in prison. Detectives were sure they had their man and the case was closed. Then, on 24th September 1974, detectives were called to a scene to the north of Florence where two bodies in a parked car had been discovered. A walker had spotted the bodies of 18-year-old Stefania Pettini and 19-year-old Pasquale Gentilcore. Pasquale was half-naked in the driver's seat of his father's Fiat while Stefania was completely naked and found at the rear of the vehicle, where her body had been posed by the killer in a spreadeagle position. Her vagina had been mutilated by a vine branch. While the young man appeared to have been shot and shell casings littered the scene, Stefania looked as though she had been stabbed multiple times. Her handbag was found in a neighbouring field and its contents had been strewn around the ground. At the post-mortem, it became clear that both victims had been shot with a .22 Beretta. The bullets proved that the young couple had been killed with the exact same weapon as Barbara and Antonio some eight years before. But Stefania had also been stabbed at least 96 times and police were confident that it was one of the knife wounds that delivered the fatal wound to the young girl. Three men came under suspicion for the crime including Bruno Mocali, Guido Giovannini and Giuseppe Francini, although no links to the murder could be found and they were all released without charge. What the police did know was that the murderer was a sexual deviant and that the first two deaths were unlikely to have been carried out by Stefano Mele. No killer was ever found.

Seven years later, in early June 1981, victims five and six were discovered by an off-duty police officer out on a weekend walk with his son. Giovanni Foggi (30) was found slumped over the wheel of his car, which was parked at the side of a country road. The police officer immediately called in his colleagues and they soon found the body of 21-year-old Carmela De Nuccio lying at the bottom of a steep bank about 20 yards away from the vehicle. The lovers had died of multiple gunshot wounds from a .22 Beretta and Giovanni had been stabbed three times. Carmela's vagina had been removed by someone whom the pathologist believed had skill in using surgical instruments. The bullets were then compared to those from the 1974 killings and a ballistics match was found. Police now knew they had a serial killer on their hands. They focused their investigation on Enzo Spalletti, who was renowned as an occasional voyeur and whose car had been seen in the area around the time of the murders. What was particularly interesting to police was the fact that Spalletti seemed to know about the car and its occupants before details were released in the press. He was arrested and remanded in custody.

Just over four months later, the bodies of Susanna Cambi (24) and her boyfriend, 26-year-old Stefano Baldi, were discovered by another young couple just north of Florence in Calenzano. The murder victims had parked their car at a scenic spot and had been brutally stabbed to death by a cold-blooded killer. Both had also been shot. Susanna had also had her vagina removed, just like Carmela, but a larger area had been taken and less precision used by the killer or killers. In addition, the victim's abdominal wall had been cut through by a single-edged knife, which was approximately up to seven centimetres long. The weapon used was a .22 Beretta and the ballistics tests proved positive as a match for the previous murders. Witnesses reported a red Alfa Romeo GT driving away at speed from the scene. The people of the province of Florence were now alerted to the fact that among their midst lay a sadistic serial killer of young couples. As Spalletti was in jail at this time, he was obviously not responsible for this or the previous murders and was released.

Despite the fact that many locals around Florence were nervous, young couples still sought isolated spots in which to make love and, on 19th June 1982, another couple – 20-year-old Antonella Migliorini and her boyfriend, 22-year-old Paolo Mainardi – were attacked by the same killer. They were close to Via Nuova Virgilio when someone came out of the bushes and started shooting at them. Antonella died almost immediately, but Paolo was able to start the car, turn on the headlights and reverse the car some distance, despite his injuries. However, these, combined with the panic he must have been feeling, meant that the car ended up in a ditch and he was unable to get it out again. The killer shot out the headlights before emptying his gun into the two victims. He must have been disturbed because he didn't mutilate Antonella and, instead, fled from the scene after he coolly turned off the victim's engine, threw the keys into nearby weeds and disappeared into the night. He did not realize that one of his victims was still alive. Paolo wasn't able to help police, however, when he was discovered the following morning; he never regained consciousness and died from his gunshot wounds just a few hours later.

In a clever move by the assistant district attorney, it was reported that Paolo was still alive when he was taken to hospital and that he had given a clear description of his attacker to police. A man called Red Cross emergency workers following the news in the papers, at first pretending to be from the DA's office before eventually admitting that he was the murderer. He was anxious to know what the young victim had said. The murderer was by now dubbed "The Monster of Florence" or "Il Mostro". Police knew that Mele could not have killed anyone since 1968, but they believed him to have an accomplice. For his part, the convicted murderer continued to claim his innocence and refused to co-operate in any of the investigations.

More than a year later, on 9th September 1983, German tourists 24-year-old Horst Meyer and Jens Rusch (also 24) were shot dead in their Volkswagen bus in Galluzzo. Police believe that the killer mistook the slight build of Rusch and his long blond hair as that of a female. Then, on 29th July the following year, Claudio Stefanacci – who was 21 – and his 18-year-old girlfriend Pia Gilda Rontini were shot and stabbed in their Fiat Panda, which was parked in woodland near Vicchio di Mugello. The female victim's vagina was removed, as in earlier cases, although, this time, the left breast was also removed. Pia had complained to friends that she had been harassed by an unpleasant man at the bar where she worked and there were reports that the couple had been followed by a man some hours before the attack. Both victims were shot with a .22 Beretta and Pia's body had been slashed with a knife more than 100 times. It was definitely the work of the Monster of Florence; however, police still had very little to go on and no new or significant clues that would help lead them to the killer. Then, the final murders by the Monster of Florence took place, in September 1985.

The two victims, from Audincourt in France, were on holiday in the province of Florence when they were brutally killed while sleeping in their tent. Nadine Mauriot (36) was shot and stabbed inside the tent before her left breast was removed by the killer. Her partner, 25-year-old Jean-Michel Kraveichvilli, was killed a little way from the tent and it appears he had been trying to escape his murderer. The killer, in a move not seen previously, then sent a note, along with a section of Nadine's left breast, to the state prosecutor to say that two more murders had taken place. The bodies were discovered by a passer-by collecting mushrooms just a few hours before the letter arrived.

A man named Pietro Pacciani became of interest to police during the eight years that followed. He had already served time in prison for the murder of a travelling salesman who had had an affair with his fiancée in 1951. His known associates, members of an occult group in which he was involved, were also described as "peeping Toms". Pacciani had married and had children on his release from prison, but was jailed again in 1987 for beating his wife and sexually molesting his two young daughters. He was freed in 1991.

Witnesses came forward to claim that Pacciani and three associates were involved in using female body parts during their satanic rituals, and Pacciani was arrested in 1993. His trial, in 1994, was televised and became compulsive viewing, but it highlighted a complete lack of evidence linking him to the murders. However, he was convicted of seven of them and sentenced to life imprisonment despite his pleas of innocence. He was cleared by the Court of Appeal in February 1996 after his conviction was ruled unsafe. A retrial was ordered on 12th December that same year, after one of Pacciani's associates, Giancarlo Lotti, confessed that he and the former accused had perpetrated the crimes. Another of their associates was also charged with murder and, in May 1997, Mario Vanni and Lotti stood trial for five of the double murders. They were convicted and imprisoned. Police believed by this time that a gang of men were responsible for the killings. However, Pacciani never made it to the retrial planned in 1998. He was found semi-naked, lying face down on the floor of his home. It was believed that he had suffered from a heart attack; however, drugs were also found in his system and police surmised that Pacciani was killed in order that the real "monster" or "monsters" escaped being brought to justice.

Police didn't close the case following the death of Pacciani and, at the beginning of the 21st century, made it public that they believed a group of educated, wealthy men were responsible for the murders. They released very little information about the new suspects they thought responsible, although it is known that they included between 10 and 12 men involved in occult activities, including a doctor and an artist from Switzerland.

# The Zodiac Killer

(1968–1969)

Of the 37 victims the Zodiac killer claims to have murdered, police have only ever attributed seven attacks to the unknown assailant, and victims of two of those survived their horrendous ordeals. The Zodiac gave himself the name when he began a series of murders in northern California in the late 1960s and early 1970s. Of his victims, four were men and three were women. The Zodiac began sending letters about his crimes to local press not long after the attacks began, including four cryptograms, only one of which has been solved.

Despite taunting the public and the police with his letters, the killer has never been found and his identity remains as elusive today as it did in 1968 when the first attack took place. On 20th December 1968, high school sweethearts Betty Lou Jensen and David Faraday were on their first date, bound for a Christmas concert at Hogan High School. However, they changed their minds and went to visit a friend instead, before going to a local restaurant. At about 10.15pm, the young couple stopped in a gravel area on Lake Herman Road, just outside of Benicia, in a popular area for lovers. They were discovered shot dead around 11.00pm by a local resident. The pathologist surmised that the couple had been ordered out of the car by the killer and that he had shot the young girl in the head first. It was thought that David Faraday received five gunshots in the back as he tried to turn and flee from his attacker. No real clues came to light.

The following year, on 4th July and just four miles from the scene of the first murder, a young couple were enjoying each other's company while parked in the Blue Rock Springs Park. Nineteen-year-old Michael Mageau and 22-year-old Darlene Ferrin noticed a car that parked alongside them but then almost immediately drove away again. The car returned about 10 minutes later and parked behind them. The driver got out of the vehicle, approached the passenger door of the couple's car and shone a torch into his victims' eyes before shooting them five times each. Michael wasn't dead, but his moaning brought the attacker back to the car and two more shots were fired into each victim. While Ferrin was killed, Michael miraculously managed to survive the attack, despite being shot in the head, face and chest. On the following day, a call was made to police at 12.40am by a man claiming to be responsible for the murders. He also told officials during the call that he was responsible for the deaths of the 16- and 17-year-old victims from the first attack. In a chilling cryptogram – which was deciphered – the Zodiac wrote:

*I LIKE KILLING PEOPLE BECAUSE IT IS SO MUCH FUN IT IS MORE FUN THAN KILLING WILD GAME IN THE FORREST BECAUSE MAN IS THE MOST DANGEROUE ANAMAL OF ALL TO KILL SOMETHING GIVES ME THE MOST THRILLING EXPERENCE IT IS EVEN BETTER THAN GETTING YOUR ROCKS OFF WITH A GIRL THE BEST PART OF IT IS THAE WHEN I DIE I WILL BE REBORN IN PARADICE AND THEI HAVE KILLED WILL BECOME MY SLAVES AND I WILL NOT GIVE YOU MY NAME BECAUSE YOU WILL TRY TO SLOI DOWN OR ATOP MY COLLECTIOG OF SLAVES FOR MY AFTERLIFE [sic].*

The shocking words received by the *Vallejo Times Herald*, the *San Francisco Chronicle* and the *San Francisco Examiner*, was one of three cryptograms sent to the local press at the beginning of August 1969, along with three almost identical letters in which the killer claimed responsibility for the shootings. He also threatened to spend his weekend cruising the local area in his car shooting individuals if the cryptograms were not printed on the front pages of each of the newspapers. The 408-symbol cryptogram had been divided between the three newspapers by the killer, who claimed that his identity could be discovered if the symbols were deciphered. All three parts were published and no further murders were committed that weekend. It was the 7th August 1969 when a further letter was sent to the *Examiner* by the Zodiac – who used his assumed name for the first time. It was the killer's way of providing details that would prove he was the murderer, as requested by the detective in charge of the case, Chief Stiltz.

Cecelia Shepard (22) and Bryan Hartnell (20) were picnicking on a small island at Lake Berryessa, which is connected to Twin Oak Ridge by sand, when they were approached by a man wearing an executioner-type hood with clip-on sunglasses over the eyeholes. He claimed to be an escaped convict who needed their car and money in order to make it south of the border and into Mexico. Believing that they were being robbed, Bryan, aware of the gun the man was holding, allowed his hands to be bound by his girlfriend (she was asked to do so by the man, who had brought lengths of plastic clothesline with him). Cecelia's hands were then bound by the man, who tightened Bryan's bonds when he discovered that they hadn't been tied tightly enough. The attacker then stabbed both victims repeatedly and drew a cross symbol on their car with a black pen, similar to the one on the bib-like clothing he was wearing, before writing the dates of the attacks underneath, on the car's bodywork. The killer then phoned the Napa County Sheriff's office from a phone box at about 7.40pm. After making the call, the attacker left the phone off the hook and it was found moments later by reporter Pat Stanley at the Napa Car Wash. A wet palm print was lifted from the receiver, but this was never matched to a suspect. Meanwhile, the injured couple screamed for help, and were eventually discovered by a father and son who were fishing in a nearby cove. While Bryan survived to help with the police investigation as much as he was able, Cecelia died of her injuries in Queen of the Valley Hospital in Napa two days later.

The next attack happened on 11th October 1969 when taxi driver Paul Stine picked up a man in San Francisco who requested to be taken to Presidio Heights. Stine had picked the man up on the intersection of Mason Street and Geary Street and was shot in the head by him after driving just one block into Cherry Street. The killer took the taxi driver's wallet and car keys, and tore away a strip from Stine's bloodstained shirt. He was seen by three teenagers who happened to be across the street and who were on the phone to the police at 9.55pm as the attack took place. The man then wiped the cab down, removing any trace of his fingerprints, before heading in the direction of the Presidio district, one block north of the crime. Unfortunately, the radio dispatcher gave an incorrect description of the attacker – stating he was black – and Don Fouke, who responded to the call, let the white man whom he observed go by undetected. The teenagers worked with a police sketch artist to draw a composite of the man they had seen, but no suspects were found. Over the next few years, more than 2,500 suspects were questioned. A letter was sent to the *Chronicle* with the piece of material from Paul Stein's shirt as proof that the correspondence came from the killer. There was also a threat to schoolchildren travelling on a school bus. The mystery killer who had, by now, already murdered five times turned his attention to the schoolchildren, saying that: "School children make nice targets ... I think I shall wipe out a school bus some morning. Just shoot out the front tyre and then pick off the kiddies." Drivers of school buses were warned to "keep moving at all costs" if they were attacked. Police were well aware that they were dealing with an extremely dangerous psychopath.

The Zodiac mailed a 340-symbol cryptogram in November that year, which was never deciphered. He then sent a second letter, relating to the taxi driver's murder, in which he claimed to have spoken to police the night Paul Stine died. Then, in December 1969, he sent a letter to prominent lawyer Melvin Belli asking for his help. He included another strip taken from Stine's shirt to prove his connection to the crime. It was three months before anyone heard from the Zodiac again. A young mother, Kathleen Johns, with her 10-month-old daughter beside her, was driving to visit her mother in Petaluma and was approaching Modesto when the car behind began beeping its horn at her and flashing its headlights. Not knowing what to think, the heavily pregnant 22-year-old pulled off the road and stopped. The man who approached her car claimed that she had wheel problems and "fixed it" for her. He then began to drive off, but stopped when Kathleen Johns' wheel almost came off the car as she tried to rejoin the highway. The man then offered to drive the young woman and her baby to a petrol station for help. They got into his car but he failed to stop at any of the stations they passed. He continued to drive for an hour and a half around back roads and refused to say why he wasn't stopping. When he was eventually forced to stop at an intersection, the mother grabbed her child and jumped out of the car, before hiding in a nearby field. She was found by police, who took her to Patterson. The man had long since driven off. When giving a statement of the events of the evening, Kathleen noticed that the man she had been "helped" by matched the description of the artist's impression of the Zodiac killer. The policeman on duty feared for all their lives and hid the woman and her baby away from the station. When her car was retrieved, it had been burned out.

No trace of the man was ever found, although letters continued to be received during 1970 by the press from the Zodiac killer and the cryptograms kept coming. Letters from a much earlier case, in 1966, where student Cheri Jo Bates was killed after leaving her student library on 30th October, were also looked at again. In the library, under a desktop, were some scribbled letters of a poem which seemed to resemble the letters of the Zodiac, with the initials "RH". It was believed by police that this was his handiwork, although this was never proved.

The disappearance of Donna Lass in September 1970 may also be connected to the Zodiac killer although this has never been proved conclusively either. The "cross symbol" he had used in earlier crimes was drawn on a postcard and sent to the police, alongside a "poem" that claimed to know where the body of the young nurse could be found. However, her body was never discovered despite the ensuing police investigation. In 1972, detective Bill Baker from Santa Barbara was convinced that a young couple who were murdered in June 1964, having been shot dead on a beach near Lompoc, could be victims of the same man.

For three years, the Zodiac remained silent, but he resurfaced in 1974 when he wrote to the *Chronicle* about the film *The Exorcist*, claiming it was the best comedy ever. It appears that this was the last letter the Zodiac would send, as later letters were regarded as copycat-type correspondence by police and other authorities alike. But, this was not the last that was heard of the Zodiac. In April 1975, British newspapers reported that police were hunting a lunatic who was thought to have killed more than 40 women. The newspaper named the Zodiac killer; it went on to state that it was thought that sex and witchcraft were involved in the grisly crimes, and that the killer was "collecting" slaves for his afterlife. The article stated that at some of the murder sites, there were ancient English witchcraft symbols formed by twigs and stones. Sheriff Don Striepeke of Santa Rosa, California, described how six young girls raped and tortured in his area could be linked to at least 40 other murders. The majority of the deaths also occurred during a lunar phase known as the "sacrificial moon".

No clear suspects were ever identified for the shootings and stabbings, although one Arthur Allen was served search warrants by police. He could not have been responsible for the murder of Paul Stine as his fingerprints did not match the murderer's and he was never charged; DNA evidence tested much later also proved not to be Allen's. Another suspect in the case was newspaper editor Richard Gaikowski, who bore a striking resemblance to the Zodiac killer and had a similar voice, but all evidence was circumstantial.

# Babes in the Wood Killings

(Nicola Fellows and Karen Hadaway, 1986)

Babes in the Wood is a term often used to describe a case where children have been brutally murdered together. This term is used on both sides of the Atlantic, but was synonymous with two little girls in Britain, allowed out on their own to buy sweets on 9th October 1986. Both girls, aged nine, were found dead dumped under trees at a beauty spot called "Wild Park" after being strangled by an unknown attacker. Karen Hadaway and her friend Nicola Fellows were initially not thought to have been sexually assaulted by their attacker, but they were left uncovered, lying side by side, following the heinous attack.

Police immediately stepped up their search for a ginger-haired man in a blue car who had tried to abduct several young children in the area in the preceding few months. A driver and car matching the description had been spotted parked opposite the shop, where the girls were last seen alive, on the Thursday evening they went missing. Karen and Nicola had left their homes on the Moulsecoomb estate in Brighton to visit the nearby sweetshop.

But the two small girls changed their minds and went to a chip shop instead, before vanishing just after 6.00pm. When they hadn't returned home by midnight, their worried parents alerted police and neighbours – officers with tracker dogs launched a massive search for the youngsters.

They were found on 10th October by 16-year-old neighbour Matt Marchant, who was helping with the search. Marchant started shouting and screaming and the area was immediately sealed off by police.

Nicola's heartbroken father spoke of how angry he was and told reporters he was too upset to speak. Both mothers of the two girls had had to be heavily sedated by a doctor, following the gruesome discovery. Neighbours had seen the heartbreaking moment that Nicola's brother, Jonathan (14), had run home in tears to break the news to his worried mother. Both women knew that their daughters wouldn't talk to strangers and neither child had ever run away from home. Karen's mother Michelle told newspapers that her daughter had always been warned to run away should she be approached by someone she didn't know.

The man in the blue car that police were looking for was aged about 25 and had recently tried to lure young children in the Lewes, Newick and Rottingdean areas by telling the youngsters that their mothers had sent him to collect them. The horrific murders happened just three years after a six-year-old boy had been kidnapped in the same area. He was picked up by three men and driven 10 miles from his home before being subjected to a horrific sex attack. His attackers were never found, but police didn't believe the cases to be connected at the time. However, the spot where they were found was close to Stanmer Wood, which had become notorious after a local woman, Margaret Frame, had been raped and murdered in the wood several years before. Her killer was never caught either.

Meanwhile, press reports three days after the girls were found stated that the parents of Karen and Nicola would lynch anyone found in connection with their daughters' murders if they turned out to be "one of their own". Police were fairly convinced at the time, seeing as there were no obvious signs of a struggle, that the girls had known their attacker and that it was someone from the same housing estate.

Led by Inspector John Rodway, police interviewed all 7,000 residents from Moulsecoomb estate during house-to-house inquiries; they were aware they could be talking to the murderer in their own home. A reward of £3,000 was organized for information leading to the arrest of the killer by antiques dealer Ken Parker, who told newspapers that: "The general feeling is one of extreme anger." A service was held for the girls in Holy Nativity Church where a frightened community mourned the loss of the two children who had belonged to the Dragon Club Sunday School run by the church. The murders of two small girls brought the council estate and police together in a way that neither side had envisaged before. It was usual for residents on the estate to be reluctant to talk to police, but now they had to if the two sides were to see justice for the two victims.

When Matt – who found the girls – spoke to the press he said: "They were like little rag dolls and one was lying on top with her arm wrapped around the other. It was a sight I'll never forget. I will live with the memory of their little faces looking up at me for the rest of my life." It had been a shocking discovery for the teenager as well as the families of the victims and the wider community.

Karen's brave parents eventually spoke of their grief in an article for the *Daily Mirror*, where their heartbreak at the loss of their daughter was plain for all to see. Later that same month, a reconstruction of the girls' last known movements were included in a *Crimewatch* programme, in which 16-year-old Tracy Cox described how she had to leave the two girls at around 6.40pm because she was expected at a house nearby for babysitting. She advised the two girls to go home as it was getting dark. Meanwhile, fibres found at the scene were being tested by forensic scientists in an attempt to identify the killer's clothes.

It was announced on 21st October 1986 that the two girls' families had decided to bury them together once the inquest into their deaths, due to open the following day, had been concluded. By this time, it was known that both Karen and Nicola had been sexually assaulted by their killer before being strangled, and police were hunting two teenagers seen running from the wood on the night the girls died. Just a few weeks later, the police did quiz a teenage father, Russell Bishop, about the deaths. After being freed on police bail, the teenager left his Brighton home with his girlfriend and their baby for a secret London address. He went into hiding for the sake of his family's safety, having been questioned by police for 51 hours, but he was due to speak to police again at a later date. Police obviously thought they had enough evidence to convict the teenager because, on 4th December 1986, he appeared in court accused of the "Babes in the Wood" murders. Bishop – then aged 20 – was remanded in custody for a week (partly for his own protection as anger grew on the Moulsecoomb estate) by Reginald Fitch, chairman of the magistrates at Hove in Sussex.

Bishop, an unemployed labourer, was arrested following the police investigation, despite his continued protestation of his innocence. He was known to Nicola's family as he had previously babysat for the family and he lived a short distance from them with his common-law wife, Jenny, and 20-month-old son Victor. But, in a new twist, a terrified teenager called the offices of Bishop's solicitor, Ralph Haeems, on 7th January 1987, giving vital information which indicated that the young father was not responsible for the murders. The solicitor confirmed that the other teenager had phoned his offices three times in early January and spoken to him at great length about the events in Wild Park on the night that the two girls were murdered, in a call lasting 40 minutes. Mr Haeems said: "My caller had information that could not have come from reading newspapers and I am sure it is genuine." The lawyer was speaking to reporters outside the courthouse at Hove when he confirmed that because the caller was so frightened he had nothing further to add at that stage. He would not even say whether the caller had been male or female, although Haeems did confirm that both he and the police urgently needed to track down the witness in person.

Anger continued to fuel the unrest felt on the housing estate where the two victims had lived and, in February 1987, a chanting mob firebombed the home of a runaway couple accused of robbing the memorial fund. The gang burst into the house of Kenneth Bass and his wife, Linda, and poured petrol around their sitting room and a bedroom before setting the rooms alight. As the flames took hold, slogans and a crude sketch of a gallows were daubed on the outside walls of the Bass home. One woman at the scene said it was a good job that the couple was away or they might have been burned along with their house.

The attack on the estate was only 100 yards from the girls' homes (which were only three doors apart) and came just hours after Karen and Nicola were buried side by side – as their families wanted. Not long after, magistrates issued arrest warrants for 30-year-old Bass and his 37-year-old wife for failing to answer charges of stealing £700 from the girls' fund. It was suspected that the couple had fled to the continent with their two children, and police were already watching harbours and airports. Meanwhile, Russell Bishop was kept on remand awaiting his next hearing, which was due later in February. Once in court, the accused man "gave himself away" the magistrates heard, when he gave accurate details about the girls' bodies, although he later claimed that he had been guessing. Bishop appeared in court on 23rd February, when the prosecution told the court that the reason he knew such details was because he was guilty of the murders. But Bishop denied murder, despite being seen at the park at the time the two friends went missing. He was also one of the first on the scene when the bodies were found and, during questioning by police, he described how he saw one girl lying on her back with the other's head resting on her stomach, and that he'd noticed blood-flecked foam on Nicola's lips. But the court was told that Bishop later claimed to have made up the story in order to "make myself feel important and look big". On 24th February, a weeping Michelle Hadaway told the court how the man accused of murdering her daughter had helped her search for the missing girls.

Bishop had offered to use his dog Misty to track missing

nine-year-old Karen as Michelle had stood in Wild Park; and when she heard the police helicopter overhead and saw police swarming across the park she said: "It was then that I knew." She described to the court how, on the day Karen went missing, she had kicked off her school shoes and changed into pink trainers. She was excited about the upcoming school disco and decided to pop along to Nicola's house before she had tea. Michelle Hadaway was preparing a chicken pie when her daughter called out that she was going to Nicola's. Her mother told her not to be long. She never saw her daughter alive again.

As evening approached on 9th October 1986, Karen hadn't returned home and, along with Susan Fellows, Michelle had started looking for the girls. A friend told the two mothers that the children had been spotted in Wild Park, and Michelle started calling out Karen's name just 100 yards from where her daughter was already lying dead. Michelle Hadaway was desperate to find Karen and Susan was also beginning to panic at the girls' disappearance. They continued searching through the night and, the following morning, were back in the park, where Michelle was approached by Bishop. He asked her for an item of Karen's clothing so that his dog could track the child. A white coat of Karen's was brought for the dog to sniff and then Michelle set off with Bishop and two other men. Michelle described to the court how she just couldn't stop looking for the children, even when she was searching on her own.

Bishop was sent for trial on 18th March 1987 by Hove Magistrates Court. He broke down protesting his innocence while his mother, a local author, fled from the courtroom in tears. Bishop's application for bail was refused on the grounds of fear for his own safety following the committal hearing in which six witnesses were called. At the trial in November 1987, the jury were told that the girls could only have been killed by someone they knew and trusted. The prosecution argued that the two small girls had walked hand in hand into the undergrowth with Bishop whom they knew well. Amid astonishing court scenes during which his family battled to embrace him once the verdict was announced, Bishop was found not guilty of the killings in December 1987, leaving the victims' families no nearer knowing who it was that had killed their daughters.

The following year, the Director of Public Prosecutions ordered an inquiry into the way the prosecution handled the case. The girls' parents welcomed the news although police refused to reopen the case without new evidence and stated they were not looking for anyone else.

In a shocking twist, Bishop was arrested after he abducted, molested and tried to murder a seven-year-old girl from Brighton on 4th February 1990. He was sentenced to a minimum of 14 years in prison the following December. However, when new legislation over double jeopardy came into being in 2005 – meaning that he could now be tried for a second time over the murders of Karen Hadaway and Nicola Fellows – the High Court decided that there wasn't enough evidence for Bishop to face another trial.

Karen's father, Lee, died at the age of 50 in October 1998; his family was firmly convinced that he died of a broken heart over the loss of his daughter. He had suffered a heart attack at the home of relatives in Brighton. Lee Hadaway had parted from his wife in 1992, just six years after they lost their daughter, blaming the stress of losing Karen as the reason for the split.

In 2004, police launched a fresh investigation into the case after it was decided that DNA testing could possibly help catch the killer. Bishop was still the number one suspect at the time and the police, who were awaiting the change in the law with regard to double jeopardy, confirmed that they were pursuing a fresh line of inquiry although it was decided that there was not sufficient new evidence for him to face a second trial.

In 2009, Nicola Fellows' father was arrested on suspicion of raping his daughter prior to her death in 1986. Barrie Fellows was later acquitted of all charges. Meanwhile, two families have had a further three years without ever knowing the truth about what happened to their much loved children. Like many other families who are victims of unsolved crimes they may never know what really happened, but perhaps, with the advent of new technologies and the advances in forensic science, which have helped solve so many crimes that otherwise may have been left unsolved, there may be light at the end of the tunnel at some point in the future and those responsible may finally be brought to justice.

Maybe, if developments continue to be as impressive as they have been over the past 100 or so years, unsolved crimes could become yet another distant memory of society's past rather than a constant reminder of how depraved certain individuals are.